Born on the Continent - Ubuntu

"Yesterday
I found my shoes.
Today
I'm here to shout about it.
For the runner in all of us."

by
Getrude Matshe

Published April 2006
by Getrude Matshe
P O Box 22279
Khandallah, Wellington
New Zealand 6004

Email: getrude@bornonthecontinent.com
Website: www.bornonthecontinent.com

Printed in Singapore. Second Edition
Cover design: Barton Matshe and Simbarashe Matshe
Cover photographs: Richard Brown, Wellington

ISBN   0-473-11020-2

Dedication

I would like to thank the force that brought me here.

A special thanks go to my parents. To my father Joseph, Solomon Bere, for showing me at a very early age that there were no limitations in life except for those in one's mind. I thank you for teaching me how to dream and how to dream big, for allowing me to be the confident little girl, teenager and woman that I am today. I thank you for showing me that the world is my playing field and that I could reach all four corners of the world if I really wanted to. And I have.

To my mother, Evangelista Bere, for being the most exemplary mother any young woman could have. As my role model you imparted onto me all the skills I now possess in my hands as well as the spirit to never give up on anything I set out to achieve. Thank you for teaching me that hard work doesn't kill, it only makes you stronger, for teaching me how to sell sand to the nomads of the desert and snow to the Eskimos in Greenland. I thank you for your words of wisdom when you constantly explained that the creator would never throw challenges in my path I could not overcome, and for equipping me with all the tools I needed for my travels - my passport at the age of 3 and my driver's licence when I was 17. You taught me always to be prepared, as luck was when preparedness met opportunity.

To my children, Simbarashe, Ziyanda and Dumisani – for your unconditional and endless love, I thank you, for your never-dying trust in my decision-making and your faith in things to come because of such decisions. You are three people who will love me for all that I am – you are my biggest fans.

To my angels, for manifesting in my times of need and despair. Some of you have been named; to those who remain nameless I apologise for not asking your names when we met for all I can do now is thank you anyway for being.

Lastly, but most importantly, thank you to my soul mate, lover and husband, Barton Sibahle Matshe, for your undying passionate love that is never ending, and for allowing me to spread my wings and fly. Without your support I would never have achieved what I have achieved to date. I will love you always – may your well of love never dry.

Contents

Born on the Continent

Prologue: The Keepers

In a far away village in the eastern highlands of Zimbabwe in Southern Africa lived a mighty tribe. One day a deadly disease swept through the village; more deadly than the black plague that had swept the British Isles in 1347 AD.

So deadly was the disease that it killed off all the strong men. Fathers, uncles, brothers, grandfathers died, leaving young defenceless widows and their children. Then the disease spread and started killing all the young mothers, and one by one the households were filled with children - children looking after children.

On the outskirts of the village lived the Keepers. They were the protectors of the land and their job was to look out for any danger or threat that could befall the village. They had built a tall platform of wooden poles, and so high was their structure that they could see danger coming from hundreds and hundreds of kilometres away. There the Keepers took turns to look out over the village, 24 hours a day, for any danger or threats. They were armed with a giant catapult and early each morning they would collect large boulders or rocks and sit on their high platform, prepared to defend their homestead. So powerful was their catapult that it could throw boulders thousands of kilometres away, so danger never came to the village.

Now, the Keepers were considered to have special magical powers, for they had the gift of vision, an ability to see events before they occurred. They had an intuitive insight into things to come. Soon they became very wealthy because they knew enough to anticipate the seasons. They would plant early when they sensed that the rains would come early and they would keep and store excess food when they sensed that the rains were not coming. And so in times of drought they had food to share with their fellow villagers, who slowly learnt to trust the Keepers and listen to their words of wisdom and advice.

When a new child was born to the Keepers' clan they gave the new life force a name, a name that signified what that child would become. And in the year 1967 a special life force was born. It was a girl, and as the elders examined the baby they could sense that this child was born to bring peace, joy and compassion to all she met in her life. She had the gift to pacify, to quieten the crying, to soothe the dying.

The pandemic ravaged the villagers one by one and soon it got to the clan of the Keepers. First the little girl's father died, and as the mother's health deteriorated she realised that it was time for their daughter to take over the keeping of the village. With all the strength she could muster the mother lifted the little 3 year-old girl up to the platform and gave her a haversack filled with corn bread, nuts, dried fruit and two large gourds, one filled with goats' milk and the other with water. She told the child to eat the food very slowly, as she herself was dying and would not be able to bring more supplies. She instructed the little girl to look out to the west, for help was on its way. Then she climbed down and managed to stumble back to her hut.

Each day she would call to her daughter.

"*Vari kuuya here*? Are they coming?"

And each day, as instructed, the little girl would look to the west and shout back.

"*Havako, mai hakuna vanu varikuuya*! There is no one, Mama. There is no one coming!"

And so it went on. Every morning the mother would shout, "*Vari kuuya here*?"

And each day the answer was, "*Havako, mai hakuna vanu varikuuya*!"

After four weeks the mother realised that her deteriorating health would soon kill her and that her little daughter would die from hunger up on the platform. She thought long and hard about how to save her child. Then she thought, if help was coming from the west, perhaps all she had to do was to catapult the little girl in that direction and she would surely meet help on the way. The child was their only hope.

Trusting her intuition, she explained to the child what she was about to do, and told her to come back with help from the west and save those who were still alive. The little girl agreed. Young as she was, she knew that this was the mission she was born to fulfil and this was her destiny. So with all the strength the mother had left in her frail body, she put her daughter into the catapult, faced it to the west and released the sling with all the force she could muster, propelling the little bundle 17,000 kilometers away from home.

Beloved Africa

Oh Beloved Africa
As I run from your shores
My heart is filled with sores
Open wounds, from rapidly closing doors

I shall miss the sunshine and the warm rain, thunderstorms,
 the plains
I shall long for sun kissed mangoes, overripe bananas
And cool sweet watermelons on a hot summer's day

Blue skies and green cornfields, with healthy yields
Crimson sunsets
And bright white smiles that flow for miles

And though I leave you, I will forever be your messenger,
I am your ambassador to the world
Mama Africa from your womb I leave
Through your warmth, your pain, you birth me
And deep, deep down within my soul,
My very being, I know I am a child of Africa

Blue skies and wide-open fields, rumbling hills and waterfalls
Your memory shall forever be etched in my soul
As I compose this sweet, sweet melody
 of my beloved Africa   Getrude Matshe, 29/3/2001

Born on the Continent

Dandelions

My religious education classes taught me that the road to heaven was smooth, straight and paved with gold but up until 53 months ago I had thought that if there was a God, she must have a strange sense of humour for I was definitely not on that road. Or perhaps in this incarnation she had accidentally handed me the wrong road map. My life had been a series of sporadic events, convoluted roads and numerous unrelated specks scattered through time. Then suddenly a fierce whirlwind swirled all around me, swirling and twirling until it blew me 17,000 kilometres away from home. What I didn't realise was that those events were all interlinked, and were tightly weaving the very fabric of my being.

My name is Getrude Matshe. I am 39 years old and I was born on one of the most fascinating continents in the world. Africa is a tough continent that can take the heart out of your breast and crush it into dust, and the sad thing is that no one will mind. That is just the way life is; no one will mind.

This book is a remembrance and an awakening. It is a reminder to people like me, people who were born on the continent; to remember where we came from. Unfortunately, when most of us succeed and leave the continent we forget where we came from, we have such short memories of what we have left behind. For once your stomach is full and you are no longer hungry; the urge to help those who are still hungry fades away. I hope my book will invoke some remembrance of the motherland and all we have left behind.

For those of you who have visited Africa, or who have lived there before, these memories are for you too. Africans scattered in the African Diaspora need to remember that we have survived one of the worst pandemics the 21st century has ever seen, the disease called AIDS. To have survived this is nothing short of a miracle. We are in the midst of an undeclared war, a war that has left Africa ravaged by illness and disease, and you and I are the survivors. We have survived for a reason.

My personal mission in this life is to try to make a difference to as many people on the continent as I can. If only I can sow the seed, and leave my footprint in the sands of time, my life purpose will have been fulfilled. I have survived in order to help those who could not help themselves - the sick, the dying and the HIV orphans in Africa. You, too, could make a difference to at least one person in your life. It could be a relative, a child or an elderly grandparent who has been left to look after three or four or five or sometimes ten grandchildren because their parents are dead. You know they are out there, you know them by name, and that is the reality from whence we came. Like soldiers on the battlefield, we now need to take up arms and fight. Fight the hunger, fight poverty, fight the lack of education and, most importantly, fight the lack of medication that is killing our people daily.

Thank you for buying this book. I don't think our meeting is a coincidence. I think you picked this book off the shelves for a reason, or maybe because it simply reminded you of home. Remember where you are from, remember those you've left behind, remember the hunger, the poverty and the hardship experienced by our people, and remember that together we can find a solution to Africa's problems.

There are enough intelligent Africans in the world today, enough gifted individuals who can make a difference in Africa, and the only way we can uplift our people, the only way we can uplift our race, is by doing it for ourselves. For hundreds of years we have sat by and looked to the west for solutions. For hundreds of years we have sat with our hands stretched out begging for world aid, waiting for help, waiting for medication to fight this pandemic that has ravaged our beloved continent.

Well, my brother, my sister, help is not on its way. Help is not coming. We are the help, you and I. We have survived this disease for a reason, and it is only through our own efforts that we will be able to rebuild our beautiful African continent. So please pass on this baton, pass on this way of thinking to everyone you encounter, everyone you speak to. Let's solve our own problems and let's solve them at a micro level by helping our immediate families, and then extending a helping hand to everybody else around us if we can. We can no longer rely on the west to give us aid. We can no longer wait with hands outstretched like the beggars we have been for centuries.

A dandelion scatters its seeds as far afield as possible to ensure the survival of that seed. A tree produces sweet, succulent fruit to ensure that it attracts birds and animals to eat the fruit and carry the seeds to more fertile ground. And so, too, Africa has dispersed her children into what we now know as the African Diaspora. I am one of those children, and so are you. We are the seed that has landed on fertile ground, and our survival will ensure the continuation of our dying race.

Statistics show that 25 million Africans are infected with HIV or AIDS. Sixty percent of the world's AIDS sufferers are Africans and 16 million Africans have already died in the pandemic. AIDS has orphaned 12 million African children.

Mama Africa has flung me 17,000 kilometres away from home and I now live in New Zealand, 'The Land of the Long White Cloud'. I know I may never go back home to Africa on a permanent basis but my purpose in this life is that of the messenger, the storyteller, the narrator of a generation gone by. I am a sower of seeds and in particular that one precious seed we all once knew, the seed called *Ubuntu*.

Ubuntu

How do I begin to describe the concept of *Ubuntu*? My personal voyage has been a spirit-led journey that has teleported me to one of the safest and most vibrant cities in the world. Before I came to Wellington, New Zealand, I didn't know my true self and my storytelling had not been perceived as anything of value. I grew up learning the craft through observation, watching those around me work hard and try to make an honest living in an environment where storytellers never got the full rewards for their efforts.

Then I came to New Zealand and, like an Olympic gold medallist who started the race with no shoes, I found my shoes in Wellington. I feel that I can win this race, I can see the finish line and victory is mine. Finally I'm in a time and a place where I can realise my full potential, a place that gives me the opportunity to express myself through the universal language that is storytelling.

My coming to this part of the world has been a unique crossing over of oceans, of mountains and of cultures, and a crossing over from nightmares to dreams. The biggest challenge faced by any immigrant in a new country is the frustration of not being understood. We create literary expression from the context of our pasts, our culture, our upbringing, and in essence our very being. What is important is that we remain true to ourselves and allow the creative energy within to flow. We have to learn to find innovative ways of marketing ourselves, we need to learn how to network and find maximum exposure and, hopefully, to fulfil our dreams. We need to learn to utilise technology such as the Internet and to look for opportunities all around the country and around the world.

Ubuntu is a Zulu word which serves as the spiritual foundation of African societies. It is a unification of a world vision enshrined in the Zulu maxim *umuntu ngumuntu ngabantu* – a person is a person through other persons. *Ubuntu* articulates basic respect and compassion for others. I am happy to say that I found *Ubuntu* right here in New Zealand. From the day I got off the plane I have met people who extended a helping hand when I needed it. I have met people who showed me the way when I got lost, and who introduced me to other people and so expanded my network of business associates and friends.

So I ask you, in a world full of people, why should there be hunger? In a world full of people, why should we feel lost? In a world full of people, why do we experience loneliness? Why should there be wars? In a world full of people, why are we still dying of this dreaded disease called AIDS? This is my question. If men and women could only feel for one another the world would be in perfect harmony and balance. If we all practise *Ubuntu* on a daily basis there should be group solidarity, there should be respect, compassion, human dignity and a humanitarian orientation in all things.

Let's go back to the way we were. If Africa is the cradle of humanity, let us learn the old ways from her. Although Africa can never go completely back to her pre-colonial starting point, we have the ability to re-establish contact with the very essence of her being. The person with *Ubuntu* is open and available to others; and is affirming of others. A person with *Ubuntu* has the self-assurance that comes from knowing that they belong to a greater whole and are diminished when others are humiliated or diminished, when others are tortured, persecuted or oppressed.

So this, simply, is my message. A person is a person through other people. Let's revive and practise *Ubuntu*

Born on the Continent

The Dead And The Dying

I have felt death's hand brush against my cheek
I have seen death's hand make strong and fit men weak
In crowded streets, I see death's face
Hollow eyes, dark deep, deep, deep
Wasted bodies...ready for the final sleep

Graveyards filled with mounds and mounds
Fresh dug graves, the air filled with tearful sounds
Hasty goodbyes, no time to weep
Behind us more processions arrive
I wish you were alive
God I pray for life, for life, for life

Orphans, widows like drooping willows
Swaying in the breeze
Give them some pillows
They're too scared to sleep, and far too tired to weep

Mourners mourn not for the dead
But for themselves, who will go next?
With baited breath, we wait perplexed

Be back next week and so the graveyards grow
Like healthy fields, ploughed and ploughed
So we can sow, and sow and sow that which we cannot ripen

Getrude Matshe, 18/9/2003

The sound of crying grew louder and louder and my little 3 year-old son came running into the room looking for me. Dumi had a mischievous grin on his face, he seemed pleased with himself. He climbed up onto my lap, cupped my ear so that no one could hear what he was saying and whispered into my ear:

"Mama, is he dead? Is he finally dead?"

"What?" I asked. I was horrified.

"Tell me, tell me, is he really dead?" he whispered again.

I looked down at my son, shocked and stunned that he was laughing at such a sad moment in our lives. But before I could rebuke his behaviour he said innocently "Now we can have the house to ourselves again. All these people will go home now."

That is when I started to cry. I cuddled him in my arms, my anger dissolved, and I whispered back "Yes, he is dead."

I couldn't find any anger, only understanding for my son's behaviour. My children had seen so much death. So many relatives had been in our home, waiting for death to come, and so many had died. They couldn't check into a hotel while they waited for their sick loved ones to pass away from HIV and AIDS, so they came to live with us and together we waited for death. The only way the children knew that it was all over was from the sound of wailing, and little Dumi knew that this signalled the end. In a few days, it would be time for a funeral and then relatives would disperse and go back to their respective villages. I realised then that my children were desensitised to death; they had seen so much of it although they didn't quite understand what it meant, for death filled all our spaces and until the sick person was dead we felt its presence daily.

We were living in a two-bedroom apartment in Bulawayo. It was small and cramped and particularly so when we had visitors as we had for the last three weeks. Farai's mother was living with us and so all the relatives who came to see him would come home to console his mother and offer comfort or advice. Right now there were ten people sitting in the lounge speaking to her. Farai was my husband Barton's first cousin. Their fathers were brothers so for all intents and purposes he was Barton's brother.

Seeing him in the hospital that afternoon was heart wrenching. I remembered how he had been crying from pain, clutching his head trying desperately to stop the pain. But all the painkillers in the world could not dull the throbbing pain caused by meningitis, and that day he had suffered the worst attack. I had never seen a grown man cry like that before and could only imagine what he was going through. What troubled me the most were his ramblings.

"Lord, forgive me!" he shouted in the middle of the night. "God Almighty, please let me live. I promise that if I get well I will change my life. Please let me live long enough to watch my children grow.

"Sweet Jesus, hear my prayers. Please spare me and give me a few more years to see my children grow.

"Lord forgive me!" he shouted, over and over. "God Almighty please let me live. I promise that if I get well I will change my life. Please let me live long enough to watch my children grow. Sweet Jesus, hear my prayers please spare me and give me a few more years to see my children grow."

Tears rolled uncontrollably from my eyes as he repeated his prayer over and over again, all night long. It was difficult to be in the same room with him in the end, particularly on this his last day. This day had been different; it was almost as if he knew the end was near.

The elders say that when the end comes we know we are going to meet our creator. Farai was brought up as a staunch Seventh Day Adventist and had, as they would have said in the church, lost his way. I don't think even he could remember the last time he had been to church, and his cries for forgiveness were a plea for divine grace.

When we rushed him to hospital again that afternoon for the third time that week and we were about to leave him, he clutched onto my hand tightly from his hospital bed.

"Amaini, please look after my children. Please, please." And as I looked down at his large, dark, hollow eyes, deep-set in a thin and haggard face, I couldn't help but sense that this was the end.

"I will look after them," I said as I took his hand. "Don't worry, I will look after the children."

I felt bad lying like that. I had three children and no job and I couldn't possibly take in another three. I felt sad that he would ask such a huge favour of me, the outsider in this family. I was only his sister-in-law, or to be absolutely correct I was only his first cousin's wife. Why didn't he ask his brothers or his sisters? And so I lied and told him what he wanted to hear, and only then did he let go of my hand. My assurance seemed to settle and calm him somehow, for he slumped back into his pillows, closed his eyes and fell asleep. That was the last time I spoke to Farai.

I was startled out of my thoughts by the shrill sound of the telephone ringing in our bedroom upstairs. We all looked at each other anxiously but didn't speak. It was late afternoon and we knew we could expect more calls from relatives and friends seeking confirmation of Farai's tragic end.

The last month had been difficult; we had already been to two funerals, one the funeral of another cousin. James had been a bright, cheerful and lively young man, always joking and looking at the lighter side of life. We had always enjoyed his visits for we knew when he came it would be a time of jokes and laughter. However, try as he did to keep smiling and joking to the end, James died. He was a bit of a ladies' man, our James, and at his funeral I couldn't help but notice three beautiful young women who attended. There were looks of disbelief on their sad faces as if they were asking themselves "Is it true? Is he really dead?" As we walked around the casket for the final viewing they saw and confirmed, as we all did, that James really was dead. I looked down at his thin, dark, ravaged face full of lesions and sores. He was definitely no longer smiling. The illness had left him small and thin, only a quarter of the man he used to be.

All these young women looked troubled and as each came closer to his casket they cried louder and harder. I couldn't help but think they were crying for themselves and not for James, as if his death was confirmation of their own mortality. I could only imagine what must be going on in their minds. It appeared that they all knew each other; they all knew that they had shared this one man, and now they each waited with baited breath, wondering which of them would go next.

The second funeral was the most disturbing I had ever attended. A mother, two small boys aged 8 and 5 and their housekeeper had all been brutally murdered. Marissa was a successful lawyer and businesswoman living in Botswana with her two children and her housekeeper, and her first cousin had murdered her and her family. The rumour was that she had offered this down-and-out unemployed young cousin, her mother's sister's son, a job driving one of the trucks in her business. He had failed high school and was having trouble getting a job in Zimbabwe's struggling economy. However, after a few months the young man became unreliable and irresponsible, coming to work late or not showing up at all, and she had eventually fired him.

It was a sad story, the kind you read about in fiction or in newspapers or watch on TV crime shows, never something that could happen to someone you know.

The day Marissa died, she had come home to drop off her two sons after school. She hadn't gone into the house but had driven back to work. Unknown to her, her cousin was in the house and had just murdered the housekeeper. The children were found with their little hands and feet tied behind their backs. We never heard how he killed them but it is believed they were strangled. Their killer then spent the rest of the day in the house waiting for 5.30pm when Marissa was due home from work. She would normally toot at the gate for the children to come out, open it and meet her, and it appears that when they didn't respond she got out of the car and opened the gate herself. He killed her as she was getting back into the car.

She was a very efficient and punctual woman, and when she didn't show up for work the next day her staff called the house and got no reply. After trying unsuccessfully to make contact with her on her cell phone they sent someone to the house to investigate, and her body was found just inside the gate. The bodies of her two little boys and the housekeeper were inside the house. It seemed to be a time for death, death and more death.

My mind had been drifting in the late afternoon sun, but the sound of wailing brought me back to reality again. As the wailing got louder the singing started - church songs led by the women. All the relatives had gathered in the sitting room and were comforting and consoling one other, particularly caring for Farai's mother who was a sad woman. She sat slouched in her seat barely able to cry. The pain of losing yet another son to HIV was indescribable. Now she had three more grandchildren to look after, adding to the other four she had already left at home, and there was a look of defeat about her, a sense of helplessness and loss. Farai's older brother had died of HIV six months before leaving a sickly wife and four children, all of whom were now living with the bereaved mother. We had all known that Farai would die, but it is the waiting for death that is the most difficult.

Three days later we were once again at the cemetery where we had buried James, Marissa, her children and her housekeeper. We had one hour to mourn there. Our cemeteries are busy places these days. So many are dying that we had to keep the ceremony brief and to the point. It was like a conveyor belt of death, one funeral procession after another. Each family was limited to an hour, so unlike the old days when the deceased were farewelled with ceremony, speakers, singing and dancing. I looked around that day and saw hundreds of freshly dug graves.

After the funeral I walked two kilometres back to where we had buried James and Marissa three weeks before. Two kilometres of fresh graves had been dug in a period of three weeks. That is when the reality of our situation in Zimbabwe fully dawned on me. We were dying, and we were dying in droves.

As I looked at some of the tombstones I quickly calculated the ages of the people who had died, and saw that they ranged from infancy to approximately 30 or 40 years. Most of the graves had no tombstones, as it is customary to place a tombstone on a grave one year after the deceased is buried. What I did see, however, were reminders of who these people had been. I saw old plates and cups and cooking utensils placed on the tops of the graves, and on the smaller graves of the children there were cot-like structures surrounding the new mounds of earth. It appeared that these young spirits still had to be protected, like children who might fall out of their cots.

Young, economically viable people are dying; children are dying and leaving a generation of elderly people, too old to work, too uneducated and too poor. Most of the elders are being left with several grandchildren to look after, and with no income and no government assistance these children are taken by their grandparents back from the cities where they lived with their parents to our rural villages. If the grandparents succeed in claiming pensions from the companies where their children used to work, and from the insurance policies of those dead parents, there is hope. The sad thing is that not many of our people can afford to get on a bus and come to the city to chase up these insurance policies and pensions, and some companies are making millions from the proceeds of unclaimed policies and pension schemes. The physical difficulties and the bureaucratic nightmare of filling out forms and supplying correct documentation such as death certificates and birth certificates means that not many will gain from such a process.

By looking death in the face and accepting its inevitability, I have come to embrace death and accept it as a crucial part of life. And so I celebrate life and appreciate every single waking moment. I realised that day at the cemetery that we were in the middle of a war, an undeclared war, and as my eyes scanned the graves and read the dates when these people were born and died I could see that the bulk of the graves were those of young people my own age. I was 33 years old. I also realised that I could be next, and that I wanted to live long enough to see my children grow to be young men and women and to see my grandchildren. It was at that last funeral that we decided that we needed to make a move. We needed to find a safe place to bring up our children, because we were in a time and place of death.

With growing despair at the lack of suitable employment, low pay, lack of fuel and country-wide food shortages, we just had to leave Zimbabwe so we started looking for a safe country to emigrate to. The United States of America and Canada were the two countries we decided to explore.

Kadiki – "Tiny"

It was 11.45pm when the labour pains started. Summer was almost over and the cool winter nights were about to begin. This was her second baby, so she knew what to expect. She woke up her mother and they set out on the five kilometre journey to the Mount St Mary's Mission Hospital. Fire torches made of grass lit the way.

Most of the villagers were very light sleepers, and as they approached the Choto village a voice called out into the dark, "Who goes there in the middle of the night?" It was Clara, her big sister.

"It is only us, Clara," replied my grandmother, recognising the voice in the darkness. "Your sister Eva is about to have the baby and we are on our way to the mission hospital."

"Wait for me, I'll get dressed quickly, I want to come with you." Clara shouted back, and within minutes she was fully dressed and had joined them along the rugged path to the mission hospital.

When they got to the Kandemiri village a voice called out in the dark, "Who goes there in the middle of the night?"

"It is only us, from the Bopoto village," Clara replied. "My sister Eva is about to have a baby, and we are on our way to the mission hospital."

"Oh, wait for me, I'll get dressed quickly and go with you," shouted the voice, and within minutes Amai Kandemiri came out of her hut fully dressed and joined them along the rugged path to the mission hospital.

When they got to the Garwe village a voice shouted out in the dark, "Who goes there in the middle of the night?"

"It is only us, Amai Kandemiri, Amai Bopoto, Amai Choto and Eva," replied Amai Kandemiri. Eva listened patiently to the exchange and wondered why no one would address her by her respectful title, Amai Bere. Everyone still called her Eva.

"Mai Bopoto's Eva is about to have a baby, and we are on our way to the mission hospital," Amai Kandemiri said.

"Oh, wait for me, I won't take long and would like to go with you." And within minutes Amai Garwe came out of her hut fully dressed and joined them along the rugged path to the mission hospital.

When they got to the Masena village a voice shouted out in the dark, "Who goes there in the middle of the night?"

"It is only us, Amai Garwe, Amai Kandemiri, Amai Bopoto, Amai Choto and Eva from the Bopoto village," replied Amai Garwe.

"Mai Bopoto's Eva is about to have the baby, and we are on our way to the mission hospital," Amai Kandemiri said.

"Oh wait for me, I promise, I will dress real fast," shouted the voice, and within minutes Amai Masena came out of her hut fully dressed and joined them along the rugged path to the mission hospital.

This went on with every village they passed, and soon there were seven women escorting one 19 year-old girl to the hospital to have her second baby. They were halfway to the hospital when the elder women in the group hatched up the plan. They were worried that the baby would come before they got to the hospital and decided to follow a traditional superstitious belief, that if you strap a rock on the back of a pregnant woman she will not deliver the baby on the road before she gets to hospital. So they found a rock and strapped it to Eva's back; adding more weight to her already burdened body.

The path to the hospital was narrow, rugged and uphill, and after walking another kilometre with the brood of cackling, elderly women, Eva decided to walk faster up ahead, and eventually she left them all behind. By the time they got to the hospital, the baby was born. Perhaps the rock did help after all. It certainly facilitated bringing the baby down the birth canal fast, for Evangelista was in labour for only 30 minutes before I was born at 3am on 31 May 1967.

My grandmother was the first to arrive. She never coped very well in stressful situations. Anything could go wrong with childbirth, especially in a rural African village, so when she arrived to see Eva holding the baby she sighed with relief. There was much excitement and commotion when the other women arrived in the ward. They all wanted to hold the baby but this little girl was so tiny that they all wondered if she was premature. They opened the wrappings and flannels and examined the little body, particularly the skin around the chest; and they found that the baby was full-term and healthy after all. She was just very tiny, weighing only 2.5kg.

My grandmother used to say that when I was born I was so tiny I could fit into the palm of her hand, and that's why she affectionately nicknamed me *Kadiki* which means 'tiny' in my mother tongue, Shona.

"All you could see were those big eyes, your small little face was just filled with two big eyes," my grandmother would say. She told me she fell in love with me instantly, and I with her. Grandparents always have their favourites and I was hers and she made no secret of it to the day she died. I was very close to my grandmother and I do believe she was my twin soul, and so I was named after her; her name was Getrude too. But this name alone was not enough for the family. The naming of a child is crucial in Africa. Many African names are not just words, they are full sentences, which capture the essence of the times that surround the birth of that particular individual. My grandmother said she called me Getrude because she wanted to pass on a little of herself to one of her grandchildren. Through me, her name and memory will never die.

Getrude, my namesake, grew up in a Roman Catholic orphanage and was named by a German monk. In German,

Gertrude means 'spear of strength'. I'm pretty sure my grandmother never knew what her German name meant.

She never had an African name other than her totem or clan name, which was *Madube*, the Shona word for zebra, and this was the name she was called by. My parents decided to give me two African names. One was *Ruwadzano*, which literally translated in my mother tongue Shona means 'harmony or agreement'. The second African name my parents gave me was *Munyaradzi*. Literally translated, again in Shona, *Munyaradzi* means 'the comforter'. To top it all off, my maiden surname, in Shona, is *Bere* which means 'hyena', and my married surname in Ndebele (my husband's mother tongue) is *Matshe* which means 'rocks or stones'.

And so I am *Getrude Ruwadzano Munyaradzi Bere Matshe,* or, if you like, 'Spear of Strength, Harmony, Comforter, Hyena, Rocks'. That's quite a mouthful.

I almost lost my two African names. Christianity and colonisation dictated the order of the day and neither appear on my birth certificate. Until quite recently most African people had to have a 'Christian name', mainly because our colonial masters and teachers were too lazy to pronounce names like *Ruwadzano* or *Munyaradzi*. They didn't even try. And so Getrude has been my name and the other two, unfortunately, have never been used officially outside my family circles.

A lot of people ask why I have a mis-spelt name. I was named after my grandmother and when she went to get my birth certificate she spelt my name incorrectly, the same way her name had been spelt incorrectly. I have never had it corrected because in my culture a person is remembered through the children and grandchildren they name and if I correct the spelling, then in a sense I will be losing a lot of who my grandmother was. Through me her memory will live on forever.

Deep In The Heart Of Wedza

Wedza is an African reservation, and from the day I was born in 1967 nothing much has changed there. Prior to Zimbabwean independence in 1980, the Rhodesian Government had forcibly removed Africans from their tribal lands, and had relocated them to reserves, or what are now referred to as tribal trust lands. No white men lived in a reserve, unless of course they were missionaries. The land was mostly poor, consisting of sand and rocks with barely enough rich soil for us to grow food. This meant that many of the men had to go to work in the city to earn enough money to provide for their families. I never got to meet my paternal grandparents, my father's mother died before I was born, she came from Murewa and the only link we had to her family were her sisters. My parental grandfather was from Malawi and he died before my father was born.

I was very lucky to have lived with both my maternal grandparents in my infancy. My maternal grandfather worked at the local Roman Catholic mission. I don't remember a lot about him, except that he was a very moody and grumpy old man. His name was Julius Mushaike, and he was so grumpy and argumentative that all his friends nicknamed him *Bopoto*, a word derived from *Kupopota* which means 'to argue'. He loved to argue about everything, even if he was wrong, so my grandparents' surname was changed from *Mushaike* to *Bopoto*.

My grandfather's place of origin is Mozambique. He came to Zimbabwe from the western highlands borders of that country and settled in the mountains of Triashill, at the highest point in Zimbabwe. This is an area where mountains dominate everything: they fill the whole skyline with the most amazing variety of colours and shapes. The Roman Catholic mission where my grandfather worked was on a hill and in almost every direction there were the most amazing views of brown grasslands and rocks, hills of bare granite, long valleys and miles of bush and low trees. And everywhere there were patches of red dust making a network throughout the countryside.

When Julius Bopoto got married he moved to Mount Saint Mary's Mission in Wedza, where I lived with my grandparents for the first three years of my life. My grandmother was a strong woman both physically and mentally. She gave birth to 11 children, and during her lifetime she buried seven of them. The firstborn was a girl named Beatta, and then there was a daughter named Lucia and three boys named Clever, Stanley and Blazio. Next was another girl, Maria, followed by a boy named Christopher, and there were four more daughters named Clara, Letticia, Aquinata and finally my mother, Evangelista. Five of these 11children died in their infancy, and the two who died later were her sons Stanley and Blazio.

Stanley was a foot soldier who fought in the Second World War. During the war he was stationed twice in Malaya, now known as Malaysia. At the end of the war when the soldiers returned to Rhodesia, all the European soldiers who had fought for their country were given hundreds and hundreds of acres of land, but Stanley was given a bicycle by the government as compensation for his service. Stanley was married and had seven children, but his life reached a tragic end when he was poisoned at a party. It is believed poison was put in his glass of beer.

His brother Blazio was the victim of assault. He was attacked at a wedding while he was trying to break up a fight, and the man who killed him struck him on the head with a metal pole. Blazio was survived by his wife and two children. His wife later remarried and again death befell the family, for she was murdered by her second husband who struck her with an axe during an argument. When he realised that he had killed his wife he hung himself. Blazio's two children were later taken into care by my grandmother.

Maria, Christopher, Clara and my mother Eva all married and had children. Maria had three, Christopher seven, Clara nine and Eva had five children. In total my grandmother had 34 grandchildren, four of whom died before her.

My grandmother used to say that I learnt to talk before I could walk. Apparently I was such a lazy little thing I even refused to crawl on my knees as regular babies do, but shuffled around on my bottom until I was almost 14 months old and my parents had started to worry a little about whether I had a disability. The one assurance they had that ruled out mental retardation was the fact that I could talk. I talked all the time. I asked questions about everything and everyone. And then, when I did start to walk, my grandmother said I just got up and started walking. In fact, she said, I ran. I ran everywhere and then they just couldn't stop me, and I have been running, running, running ever since.

I was a year old when my mother and father were awarded scholarships to go to London to study. The scholarships' funds, however, weren't enough for my older sister Patricia and I so they went alone and worked hard after college to raise money for our air tickets. It took them one whole year to raise the money. My father studied to become a chartered accountant and my mother became a nurse. They both knew that they had left us in good hands. My grandmother easily stepped in to take on the role of my second mother and I followed her everywhere. My mother had weaned me off breast milk three months before she left, and started me on bottled milk. It was difficult for my grandmother to sustain the buying of baby formula on her limited earnings, and so she gave me cow's or goat's milk.

She did have problems, however, trying to wean me off the bottle. I drank all the milk that was available until the cows and goats dried up, but I refused to give up my bottle and I would cry and throw tantrums when the milk was finished. One morning my grandmother had had enough, so she decided to put *piri piri* (hot chillies) on the teat of the bottle in an attempt to discourage me. She used to say I would suck so hard, all the time crying with discomfort from the hot chilli sauce she had applied to my bottle. When this didn't work she decided to crush my milk bottle with a rock, and she threw it into the field near the kitchen. I cried long and hard for my bottle and, miraculously, I found it three weeks later while I was playing in the field. My grandmother was horrified to find me running to her holding my broken, dirty old plastic bottle. She said I went into the kitchen and got some water and started to wash the bottle, then I tried to fill it up with water so that I could drink. By the time she realised what I was up to, the kitchen was a mess because I was trying to put water in the damaged bottle, which of course leaked so the water flowed right through and onto the floor.

She eventually took pity on me, put some water into a metal bucket and brought it outside, and I spent all that afternoon filling up the bottle with water and trying to drink, to no avail. She said it was almost as though I was convinced I wasn't getting enough food or nourishment without my bottle, so she decided to substitute the milk with unpolished rice in peanut butter sauce. It seemed to work, and to this day I love eating unpolished rice in peanut butter sauce.

My mother says she worried about us every day when she was away. Her biggest fear was that during the rainy season we would drown in one of the open wells and streams around the village. My grandmother, however, was the best surrogate mother ever. She was a gentle-natured woman who never used to shout or raise her voice, but at the same time she was extremely firm and was a good disciplinarian. At the end of each day when she got home from the field she would sit me on her lap and tell me stories. Up until the time I left for London she would take us everywhere with her and, because I was the smallest, I got to ride on her back. Even if she was working in the field she would carry a towel, and if I got tired of playing and wanted to sleep she would put me on her back and continue with her work until I fell asleep. Then she would place me ever so gently on the ground at the edge of the field where she could watch over me while she worked. She was a hard-working woman, my grandmother. She would leave home early every morning to go to the field to work. She always had a good harvest and we never went hungry.

Mhiri Kwemakungwa – 'The land across the seas'

Two years later my parents eventually had enough money to send for us, and my grandmother sadly prepared her two little grandchildren for the great trip across the seas. When they told her the plane would be in the air for 11 hours she almost refused to let us go and they say she was so heartbroken about our leaving, she was depressed for months after we had gone.

When we finally got to London, I was so disappointed because it was nothing like home. There were grey skies and cold winter days and the sun just didn't shine. When we arrived I didn't recognise my mother. She says my sister knew exactly who she was and cried when she first saw her, but I kept my distance and called her Sisi; which means sister.

"What is your name, Sisi?" I would ask.

"I am your mother, Getty," my mother would explain. She says I looked at her in disbelief and answered, "My mother has gone to the land across the seas."

"I am your mother," she would insist.

"Is that bald man your husband?" I would ask about my father.

"He is your father, child."

"But Grandma tells me my father has also gone to the land across the seas," I would reply. "So, what is his name?"

"He is Father to you," my mother would say, exasperated, but the questions just didn't stop.

"He's very quiet, isn't he?" I would say, which my mother thought was a clever observation, for my father is indeed a very quiet man. "Whose house is this?"

"This is our house, your new home," my mother would explain patiently.

"When is my grandmother coming to fetch us?" I would ask, looking at the door.

"Grandmother is not coming. Getty, come and sit here next to me." But I refused, and only started to trust these two strangers who were claiming to be my parents when my sister Patricia went close to them. This upset and depressed my mother. It took weeks for me to trust her and realise that she was indeed my long lost mother. One year is a long time in a small child's life. Up to that point my grandmother was my mother and, although she reminded me every day that I would one day reunite with my real mother, who had gone to the land across the seas, I didn't have a clear memory of who this real mother was.

My daily ritual for the next six months was to take some bread, wrap it up and put it in my bag and prepare to leave, ready to go back to my granny at Wedza. When I was asked what the parcel was for I would simply say "This bread is for Ambuya, Grandmother. I know she will like it. Right now she's probably sitting underneath the peach tree waiting for us to come back."

This was my grandmother's daily ritual. When she got home from the fields she would sit under the peach tree, exhausted from a day in the fields, and she would call out to me, "Getty, *ndiigire mvura yekunwa*. Please bring me some water to drink." And I would run into the kitchen and fetch her a gourd filled with water.

The bread was for Ambuya because we didn't have bread every day in the rural areas. If we were lucky we would eat it once a year at Christmas or, during the year, if a kind relative came to visit they would bring us a loaf of bread from the city and that was a real treat. Now in this cold, miserable place, although there was no sunshine, Christmas was celebrated every day because we ate bread every day. That's how I perceived London.

We lived in Clapham Common and there were very few black people in our neighbourhood. I couldn't speak a word of English when we arrived in London, only Shona, and I was petrified of white people. Their pale skin and strangely coloured eyes scared me. In my world everyone was black, and my mother tells me that whenever people saw us walking in the street, they would come and say hello and comment on how sweet we were and pat my hair and make me cry. It took me a long time to get used to this new life.

But life was good. They say I soon forgot about Africa and my grandmother, the sunshine, the peach and the mango trees, the watermelons and the storytelling in the late afternoon sun. One thing I did hold on to, however, was my doll. Although my parents bought me beautiful white porcelain dolls with long, flowing blond hair I still held on to Chipo, a doll my grandmother had fashioned out of a corncob and corn leaves.

Chipo means 'gift'. My grandmother named her, and Chipo never left my side. She slept with me, ate with me, talked

Shona with and to me and she reminded me of Africa. Chipo didn't have hair; come to think of it Chipo didn't even have a face. She had no limbs, either, but although she was faceless, she could speak. Chipo and I would talk for hours. As the months rolled by I started to forget how to speak Shona. So, too, Chipo found it harder to understand my new found language of English. And because most of my friends had blond hair and blue eyes and all my white dolls could speak English, Chipo was slowly forgotten and was pushed to the back of a closet. I had lost my best friend and my only link to my life in Africa.

I started going to day care. I was 3 years old and it was difficult for my parents to separate my sister and me. In their absence we had grown very close and Patricia, although only two years older than me, had taken on the responsibility of being my protector. She still keeps that role today. When I look at the photographs of us at that time we would be standing side by side but she would always stand one step ahead of me, as if sheltering me from harm, and she always held my hand.

We were severely malnourished when we got to London, because our daily nutritional intake had consisted mostly of starch. Sadza was our staple diet. This is a mixture of cornflour and water cooked to the consistency of mashed potatoes. Malnutrition was common amongst children our age. Because of the lack of electricity in the village, meat was rarely eaten and we had no way of refrigerating perishables. If on a special occasion a cow was slaughtered the meat would be cut into strips, salted and dried in the sun. This would preserve the meat and it meant we had meat for at least two to three months. It was not a common occurrence however. Cattle are wealth in Africa and are only slaughtered on very rare and special occasions, therefore we ate cornmeal with the cabbage or green vegetables grown around the well at the mission school. If any of the cattle or goats were feeding their young, some of the milk would be collected, stored in a metal bucket and covered with a lid. It fermented for a few days and when the milk had curdled into a sour yoghurt it would be eaten with the sadza (cornmeal). With the change of diet in London, it didn't take long for us to glow. The change in diet and nutrition was remarkable.

It was a difficult time, however, for my parents who were both students struggling to study while at the same time looking after two small children on one scholarship. It meant they both had to look for work after college so they could pay the bills. They made quite a lot of friends during this time; some of them people from Rhodesia whom they knew before they left home. The lady who was kind enough to escort us from Salisbury to London was a friend of my mother's. Her husband, a lawyer, had gone to London a year before, and she was following with her two children to join him and hopefully to train as a nurse. When my parents had raised enough money for our tickets they asked her to bring us to them. It worked out cheaper and meant they had a bit of money to spare when we arrived.

After three years of study we returned to Rhodesia, and going back home was interesting. I remember when we arrived back from London we drove to Wedza to see my grandparents, and my home village looked like something from another planet. I remember thinking, how could people live like this? There was no running water and if I needed the toilet I had to go to the bush and use those great big hairy leaves my grandmother thought were toilet paper to clean myself. I was soon reunited with all my cousins and friends, but now they all seemed so uncivilised and dirty. The children walked around with no shoes and their clothes looked worn out and tattered. And their hair was rough, coarse nappy hair; unkempt and unstrengthened, in contrast to my sister's and my shoulder-length, hot-combed, straightened hair. All our cousins envied us because we had lived overseas and spoke perfect English and that made us appear more intelligent.

My uncle Christopher, my mother's only living brother, would take me to the mission school where he used to teach, and show me off to all his friends and the parish priest. I remember all the teachers crowding around me when I spoke to them in English. I remember, too, the look of pride in my uncle's eyes when he saw their amazement and admiration as I answered with confidence all the questions the parish priest asked me. The teachers at the school crowded around me and asked the most obvious questions, like "What is your name?"

"My name is Getrude Bere," I answered confidently in perfect English.

"How old are you?" someone else would ask.

"I'm five years old," I would reply.

"Who is your grandmother?"

"My grandmother is Getrude Bopoto."

And so the questioning would continue. I was sure they knew the answers but the fascination was in hearing me speak English so fluently and without an African accent, for I could speak the Queen's English. One day one of the teachers said, "Boy, if you closed your eyes you would think she was a white kid," and everybody laughed. And so I became the white kid trapped in a black skin. When I look back now, I must have seemed like an alien returned to this small, quaint African village.

The way I speak and articulate the English language has truly opened a lot of doors for me. People perceive you differently if you can speak their language fluently. I have seldom gone into a job interview and not got the job.

Being back in Wedza was good but it was short lived. My sister was starting school that year and we would soon be going back to Salisbury. But while we were there we soon loosened up and stopped dressing up and wearing shoes every day, and before long the hot sand between my toes felt so good that I would run barefoot everywhere; in the fields or playing by the stream with our friends and cousins. We soon forgot to be self-conscious about our bodies and would play naked in the hot afternoon sun after we had finished our daily chores, and I remember some days going skinny-dipping by a pool in the woods.

The rat mobile

My sisters and my job was to guard the cornfield from the baboons, so every morning we would wake up and we would go to our station. This was a platform my grandfather had built out of poles at the edge of the cornfields. It was designed in such a way that we could see the baboons before they came, and first thing in the morning we would collect as many rocks as we possibly could and pile the rocks up on the platform. When the baboons came we had something to throw at them, to chase them away from eating our corn.

The worst time of the day was in the mornings when the baboons would wake up and go out scavenging for food. The adults left early in the morning, before it got too hot, for their work in the fields. We woke up at 7 o'clock so from about 8 o'clock in the morning my sister and I would be sitting on our little platform waiting for the baboons to come so we could chase them away. When they came, we were ready. We threw and hurled those rocks down at the baboons and chased them out of the cornfield. Baboons are very destructive creatures. They can eat an entire cornfield in minutes if the whole troop comes in a drove, so we knew how important our role was. If we didn't protect the corn we didn't have food.

We would leave the house every morning to go to the platform, equipped with a gourd of water and a small amount of salt tied in a little plastic packet. We might also have one or two matches that we could strike on a rock to make a fire. By midday when the sun was hot and scorching, the temperatures would be 35-40 degrees in the shade. We were tired, hungry and thirsty and, because of the scorching heat, the baboons would probably be having a siesta so we were safe. Now it was our time to eat, and we went to look for something for our meal. They wouldn't be back until late afternoon when the temperature was cooler.

The universe provided everything we needed for the day, and looking for food could be fun. My particular skill was in catching grasshoppers. I would get a small plastic bag and go into the cornfield looking for big, fat, juicy grasshoppers or locusts to eat for lunch. The locusts were easy to catch and we would place them alive in our little plastic bag. We would also collect monkey oranges - sweet, juicy fruits that grow on trees. A hard outer shell covers them and you need to smash open with a rock in order to get to the fruit, but the effort in opening these fruits is certainly worth it. Monkey oranges are juicy and succulent with a sweet, tangy aroma. I'm not sure why they are called 'monkey oranges'; we call them *matamba*. Perhaps the Europeans saw monkeys eating them and named them accordingly. During the rainy season there was also an assortment of berries to pick.

The routine was that for a good 30 minutes my sister and I would go in opposite directions. Her job was to go to the grass fields and catch one or two field mice for our lunch. Some days she could do it without my help, and on days when she needed my help we had devised a clever scheme to catch the little suckers. We invented a device which I guess I would call the rat mobile. It was a large, empty oil barrel. On the days when my sister had trouble catching her prey she would put me in the empty barrel and we would find a nice, sloped grassy field, then she would roll me down in the barrel. As I rolled down I crushed the field mice with my body weight, then we would go back and pick up our catch. We felt like little hunters.

Then came the preparation of the meal. We had to make a fire in which to roast our grasshoppers and field mice. We were always careful not to burn ourselves and in particular, during the dry season, not to start a large veld fire. The safest place to light the fire was along a path or any clearing that had a lot of sand around it. Once the meal was roasted we would quickly salt the meat and eat it, washing it down with water from the gourd. We were very careful, however, not to drink too quickly; the days were long and hot and the water well was too far away.

If it was watermelon season, my grandmother always made sure to refrigerate a nice, juicy, succulent watermelon. Now you must be wondering how she did this in a rural village in Africa, but my grandmother was an ingenious woman. Her refrigeration method meant waking up early in the morning, and before she went to the field at 4am she would get a watermelon and go to a sandy spot in the field near the house that she had showed us. Then she would dig a big, deep hole down into that part of the earth which at four o'clock in the morning was still icy cold. She would bury the watermelon, and go to work and when we got hot, dehydrated and hungry we knew where to look for her stash.   It was always in the same spot, and when the sun is scorching hot at midday, there is nothing like the sweet taste of watermelon. To this day my love for watermelons can only be attributed to those small, considerate things my grandmother would do for her grandchildren. Sometimes if there was any leftover food from the night before, such as *mutakura*, which is a boiled mixture of dried corn kernels and peanuts, we could take some leftovers with us for the day. This meal took a long time to prepare and would have boiled in my grandmother's three-legged pot for hours.

The chores and duties were somewhat seasonal. If there was no corn to look after we would have to look for firewood, fetch water, or help the boys with the herding of the cattle and goats. Late afternoon was play time and we used to play all sorts of crazy games. During the rainy season we would go skinny-dipping in the local streams and ponds. We had no toys and had to invent or make everything we played with.

One day we decided to ride a calf bareback and pretend it was a horse. The poor creature struggled to escape but when you have 12 to 15 children aged between 6 and 10 holding you down and pulling your tail you soon give up the struggle. When it was my turn to ride I got up on its back, buck-naked, and held on to its neck as if my life depended on it – and it did. The minute my cousins let go of the little calf it took off and bolted into the field, and that's where the fun began.

"*Batirira*, Getty!" my cousins shouted. "Hold tight, Getty! *Batirira, usaregere!*" they laughed. "Hold tight and don't let go."

There would be laughter, whistling and encouragement from all my cousins and friends, and the game involved seeing how long you could hold on before the calf threw you off. It was fun. My cousins and friends were cheering me on and telling me to just hold on, and I remember emerging as the victor and feeling so proud that I could ride a 'horse' better than the boys.

Ngano – 'African story telling'

The evenings were the best. We would sit and watch the crimson sun go down. There is nothing like an African sunset -

the sky is transformed into various shades of red. When it got dark, we would sit around a big fire under the stars and sing songs and play games. Then came the storytelling. The older boys and girls would tell stories and transport us into other worlds with words alone. The good storytellers would mesmerise us for hours, and all the stories had songs in them so that the listeners could participate and clap and dance. The best storytelling was, of course, my grandmother's. Every evening she would honour us with her presence and when she told her stories all the children would be quiet and attentive. She would hold us with her words for hours and although we had heard the stories a thousand times before she would jazz them up and add more details just to make them interesting each time, and of course each story had a moral or a lesson for us to learn about life. This was truly a magical, magical time.

It was not until much later in my life that I realised just how powerful an orator my grandmother really was. During these years I never realised that she was teaching me the gift of story telling, but it helped tremendously in my formative years. Later when I finally managed to go to university in Cape Town, South Africa I used this talent to make money for my university fees.

Come to think of it, I am a lot of what my grandmother was. She was very gifted with her hands and could make the most beautiful clay pots without a wheel. She was extremely hardworking and always woke up two to three hours before anyone else to go to her fields. By the time the other villagers woke up and went to work she would be on her way back home. She believed in working early, before the sun came up and while it was still cool, and she would rest during the hot afternoons before going back again to her fields when it was cooler.

"She has ghosts that work in her fields," the other villagers would say when they saw my grandmother relaxing while they toiled in the late afternoon sun. "Why are her fields so well tended when we haven't seen her working all day?" they would ask. "Maybe she is a witch, and we should stay away from that old lady."

But my grandmother would only smile and say under her breath, "The poor fools, why don't they see that I wake up early to work and then rest in the afternoon? It doesn't make sense to work in this hot sun, you get very little done because of the heat." And she was right. She had devised a plan that meant she could get a lot done while it was still cool, and then rest and do other chores in the shade during the hottest times of the day, but because the other villagers were fast asleep while she worked they all thought she had some magic tricks that kept her fields so well tended.

"They would gladly stone me and accuse me of witchcraft, instead of learning from my ways," she would say angrily. And yes, she was very lucky. Christianity had brought a lot of changes to our village but there were still people being stoned for witchcraft by their neighbours or relatives. The only witchcraft my grand mother practised was that of using her brain to its maximum capacity, and she could turn a 24-hour day into 36 hours when she put her mind to it.

Born on the Continent

Going To School

The hardest part of going to school was leaving my grandmother again when I had just found her, but I soon had to leave her. We were to go to Salisbury in time for my sister Patricia to start school, and I would attend kindergarten. When my mother told me this I cried and insisted that I wanted to stay behind with my grandmother. I guess it would not have been easy for my mother to leave me behind again, and I don't ever remember another time of separation from my mother after my infancy. And so we left her again, that tearful, sad old woman who was my grandmother. She said the only consolation was that we were still in the country and she would come and visit us after she had finished harvesting her fields.

This was an interesting time, too, because I watched month by month as my mother's body swelled with the expectation of a new baby. I wasn't sure I was going to like this baby, but I gave myself up to the possibility of being his second mother. That was the bargain I struck with my mum, and we started making his clothes. I was going on 6 years old and my mum taught me how to knit. I made the baby's booties and hats while she was busy knitting matinee jackets and leggings. She was expecting the baby to be born in January and, much to my dismay, the little bugger was born one week before I started school so my mother couldn't come with me on my first day of school. My father, however, graciously stepped in to take her place and has never relinquished this his second role as my other mother.

It was January and I was turning six in May. The first day at school was frightening without my mother. I was devastated and I cried all the way to school. My father did everything he could to comfort me but it wasn't the same without her. That new baby had taken over our lives and I resented him; his coming had turned my world upside down. I was no longer the baby. Why did he have to be born one week before my first day at school? Now the little brat was home getting all the attention. They gave him my father's name, but I wanted that name; he was my father too. And why did Dad look so proud whenever he held him? He never looked at me like that anymore.

They named my brother Joseph Tagarika Bere, after my father Joseph Solomon Bere. *Tagarika* means 'we are wealthy' or 'we are content'. Why were we suddenly wealthy and content? He was born on 15 January 1973 and he was a strange little fella. He was born with a full head of curly black hair, and I remember thinking how strange the colour of his skin was. We always used to say he looked like a Red Indian - not that we knew what a Red Indian looked like. One thing for sure was that he had the most exquisitely long eyelashes and glossy eyebrows. He was a beautiful baby and I soon fell in love with him. I would insist that my mother strap the baby on my back with a towel when she was busy, and so I took on the role of his second mum and I would feed him, burp him and change his nappy.

That was the most interesting thing, changing his nappy. My sister and I had never really seen male reproductive organs close up. We had a first cousin aged 7 who had once volunteered to show us his apparatus if we showed him ours. I think we got the better end of that deal, for we quickly flashed up our skirts and pulled down our pants and before he knew it, it was over, while he was a bit slow and we got to see everything. And now with the new baby, all I had to do was offer to change his nappy, and I could spend hours examining what he had down there. He was a happy baby, happy and content and he didn't cry much, so I couldn't wait to get home from school every day to play with my baby brother Joe.

My sister and I were thrown into an all-white girls' convent, the Dominican Convent Girls' School in Salisbury. There were only 10 black children in a school of 450 pupils. It was a private school and very expensive but my parents sacrificed everything to give us the best education money could buy. The school was nice and the children friendly enough although they weren't too sure how to relate to us. The discipline and routine were difficult to adhere to and it was run by Roman Catholic nuns who were very unfriendly and strict. The convent was a frightening yet exciting place to be and I was always getting into trouble for something.

To this day I am convinced it had nothing to do with me personally, it was my presence there and what it signified. I was like a small black ink smudge in this perfect white world the convent nuns had created for themselves. I was so different; the only black child in my class.

Before our first assembly we were shown to our new classroom and there all the children quickly paired up and made friends. I remember standing in a room full of children not knowing how to approach any of them and then, miraculously, my first friend appeared. She was a small blonde girl, with a head full of curly blond ringlets, and her name was Charlotte. I was black as night and she was white as snow, my opposite, with porcelain white skin and green eyes. I was sitting at my desk and pretending to read a book, trying to avoid the challenge of making new friends. She must have sensed my distress as little children do, for all the kids were slowly mixing and talking to each other except me. No one talked to me. Perhaps it was because I was so different, or perhaps they just didn't know how to interact with me, for we came from different sides of the track. This was at a time in Rhodesia when blacks and whites did not mix, but I discovered later that Charlotte had lived on a farm and had grown up playing with all the children of the farmhands. She even knew a few words of Shona, my mother tongue, which was very unusual for white children at that time. She said: "Are you my friend?"

And before I could think of any other answer I simply said, "Yes." With that she took my hand in hers and stroked it, then we walked off together and found a pile of toys on the floor to play with. That's how I made my first friend in school, in an age of pure, sweet innocence. As we sat down to play, I still remember the excited anticipation I felt. I couldn't wait to touch her hair, it was so white and fine, like feathers. I waited for the right moment then, when she was just a little distracted, I reached across and touched it. She looked at me and giggled, then reached across and touched my short black pigtails.

"I couldn't wait to touch yours too," she smiled, so we spent the rest of our free time playing with each other's hair. We became very close, Charlotte and I; we were inseparable. A third little girl whose name was Naideen later joined us. She was coloured, and by that I mean she was of mixed blood, half white and half black. Her skin was caramel brown and she had a head of fine, brown straight hair. And so our friendship grew, and the strange thing was that we represented at that time three distinct ethnicities. The nuns soon realised that the three of us would make a perfect example of what the future had in store and so we modelled for all the school publications and magazines. We represented the future of racial integration in Rhodesia.

Spirituality versus Christianity

I became a very spiritual person at a very early age. I remember getting the beating of my life in my second week of school. It was break time and we were playing in one of the forbidden gardens or sanctuaries the nuns used to frequent for prayer. It was the most exquisite little garden I have ever seen. It had a fish pond teeming with brightly coloured goldfish, there were little waterfalls and water fountains, and the sound of running water and the singing of the birds was like a symphony at an orchestral performance. There were flowers everywhere, mostly sweet-smelling roses, and the aroma they exuded hung in the air. I remember standing in front of an exquisite statue of the Virgin Mary and, looking up at her as she held her little baby at her side, I thought of my mum and my new baby brother Joe.

The moment was rudely interrupted by the sound of heavy footsteps. Then I remember looking up and seeing a great big, fat, red-necked old nun charging at me. Unknown to me, all my friends had seen her coming, and had scattered in all directions. Before I could even explain that I had only come into the garden to play, before I could even activate my short little legs to run, she had picked me up by the arm and, small as I was, she hit me. It was the hardest and most brutal beating of my life. She hit me so hard, to this day not even my own parents have done that to me. Then everything went black. I must have passed out for I remember waking up in the sickbay in the hands of a gentle-looking woman, another nun with gentler, brown eyes. This was not the one who had assaulted me; her eyes were a cold, icy, cobalt blue.

I could hear shouting coming from the office behind me.

"Why did you do that?" asked an angry voice.

"She was being naughty so she had to be disciplined," came the answer.

"And what about the other three, did you hit them too?"

"No, they ran away."

"Look, this is the first time we have had black children in the school," I heard the first voice say. "What do you think this will look like? It will look like brutality and racism and that's something we are trying to discourage here at the convent."

"There was nothing, absolutely nothing racist about my actions," the old nun replied with dignity.

There was a pregnant silence; and I could hear heavy breathing.

"Sister Magdalena," came the stern voice. "Times are changing, and what you have done today is unacceptable. Please report to Mother Superior immediately."

"I really think you are being unfair," came the angry defence. "These Africans need to be taught discipline at an early age."

"I said you will treat all the children the same! Now, report to Mother Superior."

A hand touched my brow, making me shrink as far away into the corner of my bed as I could. It was another nun bending over me, maybe she wanted to hit me too?

"How are you feeling?" the nun with the gentle brown eyes asked me. I noticed that she was not dressed in a nurse's uniform. She still wore a veil, but she looked different. All the nuns at the convent dressed in white and they all wore black veils bordered with white headbands. That was why the children called them 'the penguins'.

The nurse tried to touch the darkening bruises on my legs but I flinched away, feeling I just couldn't trust these strange white women.

"Don't be scared", she said gently. "I won't hurt you." There was something about her voice that was honest and very reassuring, but I think it was more her eyes. They were dark brown and their colour was so familiar, not like the blue eyes of the nun who had assaulted me. It took me a very long time to trust people with blue eyes again.

The nurse let me spend the rest of the afternoon in the sickbay, but got me out an hour before the end of the school day. After talking to my mother that evening about the incident I found out they never even told my parents what had happened, the nuns just kept it to themselves. I remember being told to go to confession the next day to confess my sins to the parish priest.

In my mind I wasn't the one needing confession, it was Sister Magdalene and her horrid ways, but when I went into the confessional box I had to say, "Bless me father for I have sinned. This is my tenth confession this month. I sinned by playing in the garden during break time."

Rationally it still didn't make any sense and the priest didn't even seem to acknowledge what I was saying. I had just been playing, after all, so why should God want to punish me for that?

"Do ten Hail Marys and three Our Fathers and your sins will be forgiven," the priest told me. Had he heard what I had said? I had been playing. How was I to know that it was a forbidden garden? What kind of God punished children for playing? I later found out that there was a sign on the gate of the garden warning children not to enter the sanctuary, but this was my second week at school and I couldn't even read.

So I went into one of the pews in the chapel and knelt down and prayed.

"Hail Mary, full of grace
The Lord is with thee
Blessed art thou amongst women
and blessed is the fruit of thy womb Jesus
Holy Mary Mother of God
Pray for us sinners now and at the hour of our death,
Amen."

Now after reciting this prayer ten times I was as confused as a 6 year-old child can get. I had thought that Mary was the mother of Jesus and that God was her husband. Now I was praying that she was the mother of God, so where did Jesus fit into the scheme of things? I was totally confused. When I got home my mother tried to explain the meaning of the prayer, but with each explanation I would ask yet another question. Finally exasperated, she gave up and told me to listen to the nuns and do as I was told and not to ask too many questions. Unfortunately for my mother, that wasn't the end of it. If anything, the lack of a satisfactory answer, made things worse, so at the age of 6, I started questioning my faith.

We used to have a picture of Jesus on the wall in our lounge, painted by my cousin Kenneth who was a brilliant artist and had managed to capture the life like image of this man Jesus. Kenneth was going through some religious phase in his life and was inspired to paint hundreds of pictures of Jesus. They were all over the place, and people were buying them by the dozen. I didn't like the picture in our lounge. It was very lifelike and had eyes that would follow you around the room, but what made it worse was the colour of those eyes. They were exactly the same as those of the nun who had given me the beating.

I told my mother this. I thought I was just being honest, but to my dismay she didn't understand me. I must have acted as if I was possessed with this notion that Jesus was an evil man, and so all his followers had to be evil; it was simple logic. My mother realised that she needed an intervention and she decided to invite her cousin, Sister Kevin, to help.

The exorcism

Sister Kevin was my mother's cousin and a Roman Catholic nun, and she came and stayed with us for a few weeks. I'm not sure why they named her Kevin. She was a beautiful woman and had one gold ring on her finger.

"Are you married?" I asked her when I first saw the ring. She smiled, looked down at her ring lovingly and replied, "Yes, I am married to Jesus." I was thoroughly confused.

The idea was that she would teach me a little bit more about our Catholic faith, but by the end of the weekend she, too, was exasperated. She couldn't quite give me satisfactory answers to all my questions and she began to pray over me every evening in an effort to exorcise my demons. In the meantime, I was having fun at her expense. My poor aunt felt challenged and decided to stay on for another month.

One Friday afternoon when we got home from school I persuaded my sister to play a silly little game with me.

"Lets have a funeral," I suggested. For some reason I was fascinated with life and death at that stage.

"Okay," my sister agreed. "What shall we bury?" We looked for as many dead creatures as we could find for the funeral. We found dead flies, lizards, bugs and two rats which of course we had to kill first. Soon we had built a sizeable little graveyard.

"The tombstones need crosses," I suggested, "and flowers." So each little grave had a tombstone and we made little crosses out of sticks and grass and so the miniature graveyard was filled with little freshly dug graves. Then we went in search of flowers, raiding my mother's flowerbeds to put a small flower on every grave. I thought it looked rather pretty, but the game was still not over.

"We need a proper ceremony," I said. I went into the house and came back with a slice of bread, a bottle of coke and my mother's Bible. "The funeral would not be complete without a church service." By the time my mother found us we were right in the middle of our church service with me acting as the priest and giving Holy Communion (the bread and coke) to my sister, and her Bible was full of dirt and mud. I had raided my mother's wardrobe and had on one of her wide kaftans which did look like a priest's ceremonial robe. My sister was kneeling like an attentive churchgoer and she even had on her head a little white scarf she wore for confession and Holy Communion. I didn't have one yet; they kept telling me I was still too young.

My poor mother was horrified. "This is sacrilege!" she shouted, "not to mention taboo." In our culture it is bad luck to imitate a funeral. It is believed that if you do you will only bring bad luck upon yourself and someone in the family might die. Quickly she entered our little graveyard and stomped out all the graves, and then she gave me a spanking. She just knew I was the mastermind of this crazy little game.

I decided then it was better to be a spiritual person rather than a religious one, and I decided just to try to be good. I believed in an intelligent God, I believed she knew what she was doing when she gave me a brain and the ability to question things around me. If anything, I would be insulting God if I decided not to make use of my brain's full potential.

I became quite close to my aunt during this time. We shared a bedroom and I would watch her every evening going through the ritual of taking off her nun's habit. It was quite a process, for she would take off each layer of her clothing exactly the same way every evening. She even had a systematic way of folding her clothes one by one, which was fascinating. I had never seen her hair before; it was always covered with a veil, but when she undressed on the first night I discovered that she had very long, soft silver grey hair. What fascinated me the most was the size of her breasts. Since my brother was born I had started to pay attention to women's breasts. Watching my mother breast feeding was quite fascinating and I thought that my aunt would probably make a perfect mother. I didn't understand that she would never get married and have children.

So every evening I would find an excuse to sit and cuddle on her lap while she read the Bible to us. The week before she left, I finally plucked up the courage to touch her breasts. They were so big they looked as if they were filled with milk, but I didn't know that this was a condition reserved for breast feeding women. I remember the look of absolute horror on my aunt's face when I touched her. I just reached up and grabbed her breasts and squeezed, giggling to myself. By the time she had shrugged me off and pulled on her shirt I had run out of the room laughing and calling to my sister.

"I touched them, Patty, I touched them. Woohoo!" I shouted, laughing to myself.

That was the day my aunt left. She never told a soul, not even my mother about what happened, and to this day we have never talked about it.

After my aunt left, the rift between my mother and me grew bigger and she just didn't seem to have any time for me any more. I became very rebellious. I found a nice hiding place at the back of the house and hid there whenever I had had a fight with my mum. I used to love hearing her calling out to me.

"Getty, *Mwanangu, urikupi*? Getty, my child, where are you?" she would call with concern in her voice. At first she was genuinely concerned, until my sister told her where my hiding place was. It was an old oil barrel near our chicken house, and I spent hours hiding in this barrel. It was a comforting place. Perhaps it reminded me of our rat mobile. Sometimes I would spend all afternoon in there and I always made sure I had some food and something to drink. The new baby was taking up so much of my mum's time and I felt neglected. Patricia seemed to be coping well with the changes but I was struggling to accept the new addition to our lives.

My father knew I loved apples and he would go to the market and buy two large sacks of apples. He would put one aside in the pantry and tell everyone that that sack was for me only, and that would make me feel so special. He went to an auction one Saturday and brought back a large box full of LPs that were of classical music records, so I got exposure to compositions by Beethoven, Bach, Tchaikovsky, Chopin, Mozart, Vivaldi and Schubert. Before long I was humming intricate pieces of classical music by heart. I always had a good ear for music and I surprise myself even now with how much I remember. I wanted to take up music but the lessons were far too expensive and my parents were barely managing the school fees, so I watched with envy as my friends attended their piano, cello or violin lessons.

In grade three I started taking ballet lessons. They didn't cost half, as much as the music lessons and my father felt it would further develop my love for classical music. My class teacher was the ballet teacher, and she was a very unusual woman for a nun. She didn't wear the habit like all the other sisters in the convent and her uniform was blue instead of the traditional black and white. She was a very graceful woman who held herself upright at all times.

"Posture, ladies," she would say. "Posture is very important so please learn not to slouch. Back straight; heads up and smile," she would instruct while we pirouetted around the room. I loved Sister Vincent, she was a breath of fresh air and I soon became the teacher's pet, following her around everywhere and looked for ways to please her. I would clean the blackboard or go and get her a cup of tea if she didn't have time to go to the staff room during her breaks. She never seemed to be stressed or unhappy about anything but was always smiling and pleasant. My friends complained that she was too strict but in my eyes she could not be faulted, she was just perfect.

Just as soon as I was getting used to my baby brother and had started to accept him, my mother had another baby boy. Now I had to deal with two little brothers. They called the new baby John Tarisai Bere. Tarisai means 'look at us'. There was a lot to celebrate with two boys in the family to continue the family name. John was different from Joe. He was always a quiet little boy and not as demanding as Joe, and in fact as an adult he hasn't changed much. I think because Joe was the first boy he always got special treatment and he knew how my parents felt about him. John on the other hand was like me, in the shadow of an older sibling. We were the two middle children, undemanding, giving and ignored. I think as a middle child you just don't know how to demand attention and so it becomes very easy to be overlooked.

Like Joe, John was very good looking. If anything he was even cuter than Joe, with chubby cheeks, and he was always smiling. Then three years after John arrived, Patrick Tapfuma was born. Tapfuma means 'we are rich' and my parents were truly proud of their three little boys. So I learned to be a tomboy and play rough and tumble games with my three little brothers. My sister on the other hand maintained her dignity and never got dirty with the rest of us.

Racial prejudice

For the first six years of my schooling I had always known I was different in the sense that I was the only black child in my class and that there were few black children in the school when I was attending. But up to that point, because I was in a Christian school, I didn't feel different at all. The Catholic nuns tried to instil a level of compassion and understanding among the children, which helped. But when I was 12 years old we moved to a smaller, rural town called Que Que. It was a mining and agricultural town, two and a half hours' drive south of Harare on the Bulawayo Road. Que Que was such a small town that if you were driving to Bulawayo and blinked you could miss it. I've always called it a 'one street no horse' town.

My father got a fantastic job there as a chartered accountant working for Zimasco, one of the largest Chrome producing companies in Southern Africa, so the move was exciting and it meant new opportunities for my parents. But for us it meant having to cope with going to school in the public school system, which was a less sheltered environment. The year was 1979 and the neighbourhood we lived in was called Fitchley so the primary school I attended was Fitchley Primary School. I was the first black child at this school, and my sister who had just started high school was a pioneer too, the first black child at Que Que High School.

On my first day at school I fully experienced what it was like to be in a minority. The prejudice of the children showed up clearly on a daily basis. They all sniggered and laughed if I walked by and nobody would sit next to me in class. I decided to sit right up front near the teacher to get away from the sniggering and the stares. I soon discovered that was a big mistake because I became the target for small pebbles, bubble gum and wet paper darts shot from the barrels of their pens and aimed at the back of my head. Mrs Morris, a stern looking, white middle-aged lady, was my teacher. The teachers in the school were all white and they all chose to turn a blind eye and ignore my pleas for help to stop the teasing and abuse. It was very difficult to try to make friends, and in fact for the first two or three months no one would talk to me. Eventually I made a breakthrough when, after three months of verbal abuse from the children in my class with no protection from the teachers, I got involved in a fight.

In every group environment there is always one person who is the weaker of the species, and in this case it was a small white boy named Devin. Judging by his clothes, Devin came from a family of very low socio-economic status. He lived in a caravan at the caravan park. I remember that his jerseys were torn and tattered at the elbows and during winter when the boys wore trousers his were always two or three sizes too small for him. He was the butt of all the jokes in the school until I arrived, then attention shifted from Devin to me, something he thoroughly loved and enjoyed.

The verbal abuse that I had to endure was horrible. The children used to call me *Kaffir*, that horrid and derogatory word.

"Look at the *Kaffir*!" they jeered. "What is it doing in our school? Go home, *Kaffir*! This is our school."

"She smells," they would say, blocking their noses. I quietly wondered how they could smell me when none of them would come within two metres of me. And so it went on. Devin was always the first one to start as I walked into a room. I learned to escape into the world of books during break time because no one would play with me and I usually opted to stay in the safe haven of the classroom alone during our breaks. It was a blessing in disguise really as this escape fuelled my passion for reading, my vocabulary improved and I was always the top student in English.

One day I walked into the classroom and there were four or five children sitting there. Devin was playing at the blackboard drawing pictures. He looked around at everybody and started laughing and said, "Oh, the *Kaffir* has come to make the room smell again," and everybody laughed. Children can be so cruel. And after three months of taking this abuse and quietly trying to endure what these children were putting me through, I decided that enough was enough.

I walked up to Devin and said, "What did you say?"

"I said you are a smelly *Kaffir*," he said, with venom, spitting in my face as he spoke.

I wiped the spit off my face with the back of my hand and said calmly, "I dare you to say that again."

"I said you are a smelly *Kaffir*," he repeated, this time holding his nose. The laughter continued; they all thought it was very funny that Devin was being so insulting. Something in me snapped. I have never been involved in a physical fight again to this day, but something inside my head snapped in that classroom and I grabbed Devin by the neck and pushed him against the blackboard. Fortunately for me, Devin was just a little runt, but come to think of it, so was I. And I'm short, I always have been. Even at the age of 39 my 16 year-old son stands head and shoulders above me, so you can imagine what I looked like at 12. I was small, scrawny and thin, and got involved in a fistfight with a boy.

Soon everybody heard what was going on in the classroom and more children started pouring in to witness the fight. By now I had him pinned to the blackboard with one hand and with the other I started punching. I punched him so hard he started to cry. I punched, and I kicked. The children were cheering and jeering,

"Hit her, Devin!" they shouted. "Kill her!" But I had him in a paralysing grip and he couldn't move. It was good having three little brothers to fight with, my tomboy ways were definitely paying off. He screamed for help and before I knew it I was being torn away from him by one of the male teachers.

"What's going on?" asked Mr Patrick. "Why are you fighting?"

"He called me a *Kaffir* again," I said.

"Devin, did you say that?" Mr Patrick demanded.

"No sir, I didn't say that to her," he replied.

"Devin, tell the truth."

Of course, Devin was not going to admit that he had said this to me, because all the children had been told by the headmaster at the last school assembly not to be insulting. I had been to the principal's office several times to report the abuse, but no one had done anything about it.

The teacher turned around in the room and asked the other children, sternly "Did Devin call Getrude a *Kaffir*?" He glared at the spectators.

"Yes sir, he did," came a small voice from the back of the room. It was Amanda Mackenzie, the little British girl who had just come to Rhodesia with her expatriate parents. I had always sensed that she wanted to speak to me but was too afraid of being mocked by the other children. Now for the first time at that school someone stood up for me and admitted that I had been insulted. We later became very good friends and we finished Fitchley Primary School together.

"Right," Mr Patrick said to Devin. "You're coming with me." At this point Devin had a bleeding nose and he was crying, but Mr Patrick pulled him by the ear and took him to the principal's office for some corporal punishment.

From that day things improved. I had earned my place and won respect from my fellow students. At the age of 12, I had to get involved in a fistfight in order to assert who I was, and that I had as much right as any other child to be there in that school. Looking back I can see I had claimed my small spot in the world of mankind. I had a right to be there, just like everybody else. Little did I know I still had a lot more to endure in high school.

Independence Day – Free At Last

"Do not follow where the path may lead. Go instead where there is no path, and leave a trail." – author unknown

The following year I went to Que Que High School, and once again I had to face the same racism that had been inflicted on me in primary school. The only advantage for me now was that my sister was at the same school. Patricia had to go through exactly the same thing, but being a very quiet girl she didn't get involved in fistfights like I did. At break time we would sit together and eat our lunch. We always had to bring a packed lunch because if we made the mistake of going to the tuckshop to buy some food all the children would gather around us, particularly the boys, and shout in horrible raging voices "Hey *Kaffir*, you dogs, baboons, what are you doing in our school?" I would turn around and want to lash out, my temper snapping, but Patricia would always say, "Getty, just leave them, it's not worth getting involved in a fight." I thought it was, but I listened to her advice and bit my tongue.

On 18 April 1980, Zimbabwe got her independence. I was 13 years old, and for the first time in my life I felt as if I had a right to be where I was. I had a right to be a Zimbabwean citizen, I had a right to attend any school I wanted, and our president made sure that every single black child had access to education. Education was finally free. I remember looking at myself in the mirror every morning and marvelling at the fact that I had a right to be where I was. It was almost as if for the first time I was truly acknowledging my own humanity. I would look down at my hands and see myself in the mirror and something just felt different. I was free, and although I didn't quite know what independence really meant, I felt free. We were no longer second-rate citizens of Rhodesia. We were now Zimbabweans.

Our little town's name was changed from the colonial word Que Que to its original name, Kwe Kwe. My father applied for the position as the town clerk of Kwe Kwe and became the first black town clerk in the country. He made history. After years of hard work and studying in an effort to be accepted as a professional in Rhodesia his efforts finally paid off. My mother gave up nursing and opened a shop selling African fabric and clothing that she made.

Que Que (now Kwe Kwe) High School was a government school that had been reserved for white children or for black children whose parents had a bit of money and now it was open to all, rich and poor, and free education was offered to children of low socio-economic status. Before we knew it the school was flooded with more black children and things started to change.

Kwe Kwe was a small agricultural town full of white Afrikaans farmers from South Africa who had brought their racist baggage to our country. Instead of learning other languages of our choice in school we were forced to learn

Afrikaans, which we saw as the language of the oppressors. We knew about the struggle of the black people in our neighbouring country of South Africa at that time, and knew that in South Africa schools were being burned down in protest by African students refusing to learn Afrikaans. We did not have that choice, however, because we were insisting on attending a previously all-white school, so we just had to get with the programme.

A lot of people ask me what our independence meant to me and I can only explain that I am glad my children were born free. They will never know or experience racism as we did. They will never feel like second-rate citizens.

Freedom meant that I could walk into a supermarket, pick any goods off the shelf and not have to go to the window at the back of the shop, which was reserved for black people. Nor did I have to wait in a queue and allow the white people who had come into the shop after me to be served first. Freedom meant better job opportunities for my parents, who were already working two and three jobs in order to make ends meet. Freedom meant that one day if I decided to study at university there would be scholarships available for me to get a higher education if I wanted it. Independence gave me choices; choices I would otherwise never have had.

I could choose to participate in any school activity I wanted, so I threw myself into every activity the other black children didn't have the courage to participate in. I joined a speech and drama class and I was part of every single theatrical production the school staged, from The Merchant of Venice and Romeo and Juliet, to South Pacific and Gregory's Girl. I auditioned to take part in the national speech festival, too. My father encouraged me to do this. He told me to learn to stand and talk in front of people. "Then when you start looking for a job it will be easy because you won't have a fear of speaking in front of people," he would say, and I followed his advice and have never regretted it. My confidence and ability to speak in front of crowds has presented me with numerous opportunities in life, particularly in leadership positions.

My father's new job meant he was hardly ever home, but although he was always busy he found time to attend every single competition I participated in. If he was late, all I had to do was look at the back of the school hall and there he would be, standing proudly, smiling encouragingly. He is a very special father.

Before I knew it, my speech and drama teacher realised that I was talented and instead of competing in the junior section of the school competitions I was pushed up to compete in the senior section. The only competitor I had was a boy by the name of Eunis Ishmail, an Indian boy who was in the sixth form. I was only in form one at the time but we won the local competitions and went on to compete in the national finals together. He came first, and I came second. We were like chalk and cheese, for he was tall and slender and 18 and I was small and tiny and only 13. We were so different people used to laugh when we went up onto the stage to give our presentations, and I fear my smallness overshadowed his victory.

I also joined the hockey and tennis teams and for the next three years I was the only black girl to play these sports. My high school days were the most challenging and interesting of all.

I remember my form three English literature teacher Mr Davies, a tall, thin man with shaggy brown hair and brown eyes who always seemed to look scruffy, even first thing in the morning. Mr Davies came from England and he helped to cultivate the passion and the love I have for English literature. He introduced us to African literature and the writings of famous African authors like Ngugi wa Thiong'o and Chinua Achebe. Later I studied their work for my A level literature exams, and their writing helped to clarify in my mind the effects colonialism had on my people.

We were living in a post-colonial era and the effect and impact of the English language, which was brought to Africa, was considerable. They addressed the implications, and the way English had affected the intellectual make-up of the African people. In his book *Decolonising The Mind*, Ngugi teaches about the effects of the British Empire and how Europe had tried to plant its memory on the newfound landscape by exploration and by naming places. For example, in the United States, place names like New York, New Jersey, New

Cleveland, New England and New Orleans were an effort by the British to erase the old names and establish the new. So the previous memory, pre-New York, is no longer there and New York becomes the starting point and the foundational memory of that place.

In Zimbabwe we were taught in our history class that David Livingston discovered the Victoria Falls in 1855. But what was it called prior to that date? He did not discover it; he was the first white man to see it but he did not discover it. It was always there and it was called by the local Batonga people *Mosi-Oa-Tunya,* 'the smoke that thunders'. That name has now been lost in history and it is difficult to bring it back. Even 20 years after Zimbabwean independence the fear is that people will not know what we are taking about if the name is restored; hence the new memory becomes the foundational memory of that place. It is still Victoria Falls instead of Mosi-Oa-Tunya.

In South Africa, the Eastern Cape is a very interesting place because that one small area has produced some of the most leading and intelligent intellectuals since the 19th century. Nelson Mandela, Thabo Mbeki and Oliver Tambo, for example, all came from that area. But when you look around, what towns do you find there? King Williams Town, Rhodes, Queenstown, Grahamstown, East London, Port Alfred, and Port Elizabeth. So one has to question, where is Mandela, where is Mbeki or Tambo? There is nothing in the memory of that landscape that in any way points to the rich intellectual history of Africa. The works of these post-colonial writers made me aware at a very early age of the effects of colonialism on the territories the British invaded.

Colonialism brought with it a lot of confusion and division amongst African people. It brought the concept of borders and boundaries, which in the beginning did not exist. It highlighted our tribal differences and so, through divide and rule, brother began to fight with brother, fathers began to fight with sons, mothers fought with daughters, sisters with sisters until we developed the concept of our tribal differences.

Most African languages do not have the words 'uncle', 'auntie' or 'cousin'. For example, in my native tongue Shona I address my mother as *Amai*, meaning 'mother', and my father as *Baba* which means 'father'. But my mother's older sister is *Amaiguru*, 'big mother'; her younger sister is *Amainini* meaning 'small mother'. My father's older brother is *Babamukuru*, 'big father' and his young brother is *Babamunini*, 'small father'. My cousins, male or female, are *Mukoma* which means 'big brother/sister' if they are older or *Munin'ina* which means 'small brother/sister' if they are younger. I learned a lot about my language and culture while I was in high school.

Kwe Kwe is a very hot town; temperatures can go up to 35 to 40 degrees in the shade. None of our classrooms were air-conditioned so we had to study in very hot conditions. When Mr Davies came to our high school he was horrified that the children were forced to attend class in the closed classrooms where there was no fresh air and it was difficult for us to concentrate on what was being taught, and he insisted on teaching English outside. The very first day he suggested this, he read some First World War poetry by Wilfred Owen. I remember him telling us to sit underneath a tree, and to lie down and look up at the clouds while he read to us, and from then the seed was sown. The imagery created by the intricate weaving of words fascinated me and my passion for poetry and for English literature has never died.

"Red lips are not so red as the stained stones kissed by the English dead," he would recite, and I could visualise in my mind's eye the English soldiers on the battlefields of World War One. He had a way with words, our Mr Davies, and I am truly thankful that he came into my life when he did.

My high school years were very, very memorable; I came out of high school with achievement after achievement after achievement, particularly in the arts. I had always thought I would become a lawyer or I would go into performing arts or do something artistic, but that was not to happen until much later in my life.

Illness in the family

When I was 14, our lives were turned upside down by the illness of my older sister Patricia. She had a routine appendectomy that went wrong. The week after the operation she became very ill, although the surgeon who had removed her appendix said there was nothing wrong with it. She had to go back to the operating theatre a week later when she developed an abdominal obstruction – her intestines had twisted, causing her bowels to constrict and develop gangrene. She had to be operated on again and again until after four operations she finally regained her health.

My sister almost died during this time. She lost a lot of weight and by the time she came out of hospital she was a shadow of the girl she was when she went in. I had to grow up really fast too, and to learn to take care of my little brothers while my parents were away in Harare with Patricia in the hospital, so I assumed the role of the older sister until she was better again. It helped me to mature really fast. I realised that life was really short and that death could have claimed her young life before it had even begun.

Soulmate

"A soulmate is someone who has locks that fit our keys, and keys to fit our locks." – Richard Bach

I first met Barton when I was 17 years old. I remember him clearly as a damned good-looking boy who came to our sleepy little town of Kwe Kwe during his university vacation. He was a second year medical student then, and because Kwe Kwe was so small you knew at once if anyone new came to town. The first day I saw him, he walked past my mother's shop. He was walking with his brother whom I recognised, for he worked for the local electricity company just across the street. They were very different, these two brothers. Barton was tall, dark and handsome, while his older brother was shorter and had a fairer complexion.

Barton was dark, chocolate brown and absolutely gorgeous. As they walked past our shop I tried to avoid eye contact and pretend I hadn't been watching him as he crossed the street. Later he told me that he would drop his glance as soon as he saw my head come up. We played this game for a couple of weeks, but eventually I bumped into him one day at the local bakery on a Sunday morning. I had gone with my sister's boyfriend to buy some bread, and there he was in all his glory coming out of the bakery with his brother. Barton knew my sister's boyfriend because they had grown up together in

Shurugwi, a small town about 200 kilometres away from Kwe Kwe. We were introduced but I don't think Barton was paying much attention, for when I tried to get hold of him later he said he couldn't remember who I was. For my part, I still remember my heart pounding in my chest as we stood at the end of the street shaking hands. I didn't want to let go of his hand, but a part of me knew that I couldn't hold on to it forever, so we went our separate ways.

This was not to be my only meeting with Barton, as later I saw him almost every day walking past my mother's shop and, as usual, I pretended that I wasn't interested. I tried to get more information about him from one of his cousins who was in my class at school. I asked her to introduce us, but funnily enough she wasn't very keen to do so, and she kindly informed me that he already had a girlfriend in Harare and he wouldn't be interested. That didn't stop me. I went home that day and told my mum that I had seen the most gorgeous boy and I didn't know what to do. I knew his name was Barton Matshe and I knew he came from Shurugwi. My mother had never seen me so infatuated before and she only laughed at my distress.

That same week he disappeared without a trace. I knew he must have left town, so I panicked. I pulled out the telephone directory and looked up his surname in Shurugwi. There were two numbers listed so I dialled the first one and prayed. First time lucky – I got the right number and his sister Thoko picked up the phone.

"Can I speak to Barton Matshe please," I asked calmly. "My name is Getrude and I'm calling from Kwe Kwe."

"Hold on, I'll call him," she said. So at least it was the right number, I thought as I waited for him to come to the phone. My heart was pounding. But when he came to the phone, he didn't know who the hell was calling. He told me again, years later, that when I explained who I was he couldn't even put a face to my name.

"Hi, my name is Getrude Bere, we met in Kwe Kwe a few weeks ago while you were here on holiday." I speak very fast when I'm nervous.

"Ahh, hi, how are you?" Barton said, but I could hear the hesitation in his voice and I knew he didn't know who I was. I decided to get straight to the point.

"I was wondering, if you were ever coming back to Kwe Kwe, I'd like to invite you out for a drink," I said in a hurry. There was a pregnant pause;

"Oh, ahh, sure, that would be nice," he said politely. "Give me your number and I'll call you when I come back to Kwe Kwe next week." I gave him my number and we set a time and place to meet. I prepared with great excitement for this date. It was the longest week I have ever spent waiting. I had no idea then that he would someday be my husband.

I met him in town, very near my mother's shop, and we walked together down to the local Whimpy where we ordered some hamburgers and ice-cold drinks. I don't remember how fast that date went, I couldn't even swallow the food that I was eating, I was so excited, but I had to try and keep my cool. He sat in silence while I talked for a good two hours; a bad habit I had developed when I was nervous, but he was happy just to sit there and listen to me chatter on. I made a date to see him the next day, and this time we went to the local movie theatre to watch a film together. It was nice and I could tell he liked me, although he was very, very shy. He didn't even hold my hand during the movie. I dared not make the first move, what would he think of me if I did? I definitely didn't want to scare him off by coming on too strong.

By the third date I knew this was the boy I wanted to show to my parents. I invited him home and introduced them, and my mother was suitably impressed. He was a decent boy, very polite, soft-spoken and well mannered. My father, on the other hand, was not very impressed. I was only 17, he growled, why was I bringing a boy home? It was funny how my father never saw me as a young woman who was growing up. My sister Patricia had brought her boyfriend home and he had never said a thing, but he had always been a little over-protective of me.

Barton was nothing like our local boys. Most of them were rough and tough. Most of them had no manners at all, but he was really a gentleman and he treated me like a lady. We were walking in our orchard, picking fresh mangoes and guavas from the trees, and I remember an aeroplane flying above us. I looked up when I heard the sound, and that was when he gently planted his first kiss, very well timed, sweet, long and memorable. I hoped I could hold on to that moment for the rest of my life and that was the beginning of a budding and passionate romance.

On our fourth date we decided to go to the local drive-in with my sister and her boyfriend. They wanted to sit outside the car so they pulled out their blanket, spread it in front of the car and watched the movie, giving us some privacy. I remember we watched the movie Scarface, with Al Pacino, but I can tell you that to this day I don't know what the hell that movie was all about. I didn't pay any attention; all I could think of was this gorgeous boy sitting next to me.

The holiday was almost over and he went back to university and I went back to high school and, unfortunately for me, after a while I made a decision that I wanted to end the relationship. We did not meet again until I was 19 and working in Harare.

Don't Waste Money On A Girl Child

"When you have gone so far that you can't manage one more step, then you've gone just half the distance that you're capable of." – Greenland proverb

When I was 18 years old my father lost his job and the bank was about to repossess our house. Dad had always encouraged me to go for job interviews during the school holidays, again as a way of gaining confidence. He said that when the time came for me to look for a job, if I knew how to stand in front of white people I would get the work. Corporate Zimbabwe still had not changed for blacks after independence.

That holiday I went to Harare attended five job interviews and had three job offers. I could have been an air traffic controller or a nurse, but the job I took up was as a trainee computer programmer for Lonrho Computer Services, one of the largest conglomerates in Zimbabwe at the time. Lonrho paid you $500 a month as they trained you, which at the time was a lot of money, so I quit high school before I had finished and started working as a Cobol programmer. I sent every cent home to my parents, and with my first payslip we secured the 10-acre piece of land where they still live today. My mother still grows fruit and vegetables there and sells her market gardening produce.

Reunion

It was my sister who was instrumental in bringing Barton and me together again. Patricia knew how miserable I was. After one disastrous relationship I knew I had made a mistake and there was no going back. My sweet, kind sister manoeuvred a date with Barton for me. I think initially he only came to see me out of pity. I'm not exactly sure what she told him, but she must have told him that I was extremely depressed, and I was. Once again on that first date I was as nervous as ever, and I chattered through the whole lunch break while he, as usual, sat quietly and patiently just listening to me. I'm not sure how he could put up with so much chatter, but that was the real beginning of a beautiful relationship.

Barton wined me and dined me for the next two years, and it was at that point that we really became soulmates. We went everywhere together, we spent our weekends together, and we were inseparable, much to the displeasure of all of our friends and family. Our relationship was so serious it made everybody feel uncomfortable; everybody wondered how we could spend all those hours just being together. I would meet him on a Friday after work, go to his place for the whole weekend, and go back home on Sunday. I was truly in love with Barton Matshe.

I worked for my parents for two years, making sure they had everything they needed. I started a dressmaking business so that I could send my whole paycheck home for them to pay the bills and I made enough money from my dressmaking business to survive. I joined the Zimbabwe Association of Community Theatre and was encouraged to form an all-women theatre group. I called it Just For Women Theatre, and we worked primarily in our rural community teaching the rural women about HIV and AIDS. The disease had just hit Zimbabwe and WHO would come to our villages and drop flyers telling people to use condoms and to practise safe sex. Unfortunately, most of our rural population were illiterate so it was a total waste of time and money.

I formed the theatre group with a group of girlfriends and we would meet in the evenings after work and would work on plays that were related to an AIDS or HIV theme. We approached the Minister of Health and teamed up with their counsellors and educators and we all went to the villages in the weekends. We performed our plays and the Ministry of Health held workshops to help our rural population to understand what HIV was all about. This was a very fulfilling time for me because I got to travel to some of the most remote areas around the country and participate in something that was really worthwhile. Not only that, I had an opportunity to continue my love for theatre and acting and playwriting. I'm not sure how I managed to get everything done. I had a full-time job (which I hated) and a part-time job making clothes for people and then the theatre group, but it was all worthwhile.

At the end of two years my father was back on his feet. He had started his own management consultancy business, and my mother had opened a restaurant. I decided that since I had also been working by correspondence to get my A levels, which I passed, it was time for me to start on a university degree and I prepared to leave for the United Kingdom. The decision didn't come very easily. For a start I felt as if I was deserting my parents because they needed me financially. Although I knew that they were now financially stable, it still didn't feel right to leave them. And then I had discovered that I wasn't actually enjoying what I was doing. I was an average computer programmer and I wasn't passionate about my job, I did it because it paid the bills. I remember sitting in my office one day, scribbling on a piece of paper, Is This The Life You Want To Live? NO, it isn't. Is This The Life You Want To Live? NO it isn't!

I must have written on this paper at least a thousand times over a period of one week, and I finally realised that what I was writing was the truth. I was not happy and this was not the life I wanted to live. I wanted to go and get a university degree. So I wrote my resignation letter one Friday afternoon and handed it to my boss and with my last paycheck I bought an air ticket to London.

I explained my decision to my parents and told them what I had done, I wanted to go to the England to study. My father was supportive, as he always was in everything I did. My mother was a little disappointed that I wasn't going to stay home and that I wanted to go out into the big wide world on my own at that tender age. So the whole family, including all the extended family, got involved in making this decision. Many of my relatives advised my father not to waste money on a girl.

"What if she gets pregnant?" they said in one of the family meetings.

"What if she doesn't pass the exams? Think of all the money you will be wasting."

"What if she lets you down and just doesn't finish this degree?"

"Keep the money for the boys," they advised. In Africa it is not considered economic or wise to educate a girl child, and at that time I had three younger brothers. The belief is that a girl will get married and leave the homestead while boys are more likely to stay and take care of the parents in their old age. It made economic sense to keep what little money my parents had for my three younger brothers.

Fortunately for me, my father was extremely grateful for everything I had done to get him back on his feet. He stood his ground and said, "No, Getrude is going to university, I don't care what it takes. This child has sacrificed everything for us to be where we are now. Getrude is going to university, there's no debate." He basically just put his foot down and didn't listen to any of the advice he was given by his relatives. He sold all his cattle to get me to the United Kingdom. We managed to raise a thousand pounds at the cattle sale, and off I went to London with a thousand pounds in my pocket.

The most painful part of the whole journey was leaving my beloved Barton behind. Barton knew how hard I had worked to get to this point. I had studied by correspondence to complete my high school A levels and passed, despite holding down a full-time job. He knew how much I wanted a college degree and so he encouraged me to follow my dreams and he promised to come and see me in London.

London again

The day I arrived at Heathrow airport the weather was cold, the wind was nippy and the chill in the air reminded me how far away from home I was. It was difficult to adjust to the changes, because everything I had imagined about London was not true. Growing up in Africa, I had been led to believe that the streets of London were paved in gold. I had high expectations of clean, glistening, shiny streets but when I got there I was met with dingy, grey skies, filthy streets and houses that piled up one on top of the other as far as the eye could see. Everything was dull and grey, and the sun just didn't shine.

I was picked up at the airport by some old family friends, a very nice couple who had agreed to put me up for a few days until I found something to do. Bernard and Margaret were personal friends of my parents who had met them when they studied in London nearly 20 years earlier. The assumption was that I would stay with them for a while until I was settled and had enough money to look after myself, but I stayed only two weeks and at the end of that time I decided to go out and look for a place to live.

For the first time in my life I was in an environment where I could not look out into the horizon and, like a trapped animal in a cage, I had to learn to navigate without using my sight. Whenever I sat in the London underground and looked up at the map to see where I was going it was difficult to try and relate to where I was, where I had come from. The people were different in London. It's a cold, heartless society, and for the first time in my life I was amongst people who did not make eye contact. People would walk around with their heads down trying by all means to avoid any type of contact with the next person coming towards them. I remember sitting in the tube on my way to college every morning, and watching people. I love watching people and in this strange place I found it interesting to watch so many people trying desperately to avoid each other.

This was a city filled with millions and millions of people, all individuals, all trying to find a space for themselves. They would sit in the train looking down at their newspapers, trying by all means not to look at the next person, trying by all means not to brush or touch shoulders with them. Even when the lights flickered on and off they would all keep their heads bent pretending to read. I found it fascinating, it was very strange behaviour indeed. At home if you sat in a bus, you would have a conversation with the person next to you or at least acknowledge their presence with a greeting. Now in this city filled with millions of people I felt completely alone.

Overseas scholarships were hard to get and I didn't have a place at university or college to go to, so the day after I arrived in London I pulled out the Yellow Pages and I started calling all the colleges and universities. Fortunately for me it was the beginning of the new academic year and I had arrived just in time, so I sent out my applications and waited hopefully for a positive response. It came quickly and by the end of the second week I was registered at Southbank Polytechnic in Vauxhall, South London, to do a Business Studies degree. My heart pounded as I stood in that massive registration queue. This was what I wanted, this was the opportunity I had been pursuing all my life. I went back home that night feeling satisfied with myself, I had hit the ground running. Within two weeks of my arrival in London I had a place to study. I had a place where I could develop my mental intellect, where I could finish off where I had left off by leaving school early.

Finding somewhere to live turned out to be easier than I expected, for after an hour standing in the student union at Southbank Polytech I met a young woman who became my flatmate. Mary was standing in the queue in front of me. She was from Gambia so I guess the first thing that attracted her to me was that we were both African.

"Where are you from?" she asked.

"I come from Zimbabwe, and I am looking for somewhere to stay," I answered. "Where do you come from?"

Mary was British but she originally came from Gambia. She had come to London at a very early age with her mother who married a British man.

"I'm here to advertise a room that my half-sister and I are leasing out," she told me. "We found an apartment in Vauxhall and we're looking for someone to share, so I'm here to advertise it in the student union newspaper. The apartment is three bedrooms and you can have one if you like, saves me wasting time advertising."

"Really?" I asked in disbelief. "How much will it cost per week?"

"Fifty pounds," she said. "Do you want it?"

"Yes, yes." I accepted gladly. Sometimes things just have a way of working out perfectly. I couldn't believe my luck. That week I moved in with Mary and Sheila, and got a small room which I paid 50 pounds a week for. I could barely fit my single bed and a desk in it, but I was grateful to have a place of my own.

I soon realised that I wasn't going to survive for very long on my thousand pounds, so I looked for some work and found a job cleaning offices in the early mornings. I went to work at three in the morning and finished at eight. At nine o'clock I attended my lectures, and I would be in college until four o'clock in the afternoon. After that I went to Oxford Street where I worked in a bookshop called WH Smith. I worked in the music department selling CDs and tapes and the job was quite flexible. They would let me come in any time after college and I worked until they closed the shop at 9pm. It was exciting and thrilling at the same time. I enjoyed the Oxford Street job because all day, from 4pm until 8pm, I listened to music. Sometimes I'd play music that reminded me of home, and towards the end of my evenings I would play a CD by Fleetwood Mac called Albatross. It so reminded me of Barton, it's one of his favourite songs.

I found that I could fit in a third job if I got out of WH Smith at 9pm and took a short half-hour break. I found work cleaning the kitchen at McDonalds right next door from 9.30pm to 10.30pm. This last job was great. Although it didn't pay very well I got to eat as much as I wanted while on the job. It was a good thing that I had to do a lot of walking between my three jobs, otherwise I would have packed on a lot of weight from eating all that junk food and there was a limit to how much McDonalds I could take. After two weeks I didn't want to eat the food but I had no choice. And so I would get home at 11pm every night and then do it all over again the next day. I only survived three months.

The Christmas surprise

I had been in London three months and those three months went by in a blur. I can't actually remember what happened from day to day because I was so tired and so stressed out the days just seemed to merge into each other. Then it was the week before Christmas, there was a buzz in the air, people were shopping and the students were getting ready to go home for the Christmas holiday. I couldn't afford to go back to Africa so I had to stay behind and keep working to try to raise more money for my next term's fees. Mary and Sheila went home to Wales for Christmas, so I was left in our large, three-bedroom apartment on my own.

Soon it was the day before Christmas, 24 December, and I had volunteered to work all day at WH Smith. The shop closed late so all the people who wanted to do their last minute shopping could come in and buy. When I got home it was dark, cold and miserable, and there was no one there to celebrate Christmas with me.

On Christmas Day I woke up to the sound of the doorbell. Who could that be, I wondered? Everybody had gone. I knew that our landlord Daud who lived on the ground floor had gone away for the holiday, and the boys who lived on the second floor had all gone away. I was alone in the house. I ran down the stairs and opened the door – and what a surprise. Standing at the door was my boyfriend Barton.

I couldn't believe it. He had to shake me for me to realise that I wasn't dreaming; he was really there, he was there in London. I jumped into his arms, he kissed me, and I knew it was going to be a wonderful, wonderful Christmas. And it was. We didn't have much money but with the little we had we had a really, really good time. He stayed for two weeks and I remember on New Year's Eve walking through Oxford Street watching people from all walks of life and every nationality, celebrating the night. Everybody took to the streets in London at New Year's Eve, and it was a time for hugging strangers, strangers kissing strangers. We walked through Trafalgar Square and Oxford Street and it was alive and buzzing with people.

"Happy New Year," people would say. They would come up to you and hug you and kiss you and grab you, it was just a time for celebration.

But after two weeks Barton had to go back to Africa. It was a depressing time because it had been so nice to see him, and I was left alone again. Mary and Sheila didn't come back until mid January. But four weeks after Barton went back to Africa, I started to feel extremely unwell. I would wake up in the morning and start vomiting, run to the toilet and throw up. I wasn't sure what was wrong with me, I wasn't sure what it was that I had eaten that upset me so much.

When Mary came back she said to me, "Getrude, Barton was here, do you think you might be pregnant?"

"Pregnant?" I said. "No, no, that's not possible – I can't be pregnant." But Mary was a nurse so she knew all the signs and symptoms.

"I suggest you go for a pregnancy test," she said, and the next day I did. I couldn't sleep all night, thinking of the possibility that I could be a mother.

For some reason, the only thing that came into my mind was, what would the baby look like? Would it look like me or would it look like Barton? It didn't really matter, my fascination at that point was that I had managed to create another human being, and that little human being was possibly growing in my stomach every single minute that I thought about it. I went to the campus clinic and submitted my urine for the test. When the lady who was looking after me came back with a positive result, she had a grim look on her face.

"You are definitely pregnant, what do you want to do?" she asked. I remember looking at her and thinking what does she mean, what do I want to do? I was keeping my baby and I was extremely upset and defensive that she would even suggest that I had another alternative. "What I mean is, do you want to have an abortion?" she said kindly, "because if you do, you could go into the next room. By 2 o'clock it will all be over and you can go home."

I looked at her and said, with conviction and passion, "I'm keeping my baby. I'm not having an abortion." My reaction threw her a little, because I remember her looking at me, puzzled and then she started to smile. She came around from behind her desk, put both arms around me and said,

"Young lady, you are going to be okay." She held me tight and said, "I see so many confused, pregnant young women in the clinic, but your conviction is going to take you a very long way. Good luck, and take care of yourself and that baby."

At that point I started to cry for I knew that my whole life, would never be the same again. What was I going to do? I hadn't completed my university degree, I didn't have any money, I couldn't go back home, what was I going to do? But there was something about the way she reassured me that made me believe that I was going to be all right and that keeping my baby was the right decision to make. I always say that was probably the one point in my life where God touched me or made me aware of her existence through people. I kept thinking I was going to be fine, I was going to find a way out of this problem and this dilemma.

As I walked home from the campus clinic I started to imagine what my baby would be like. Of all things, I started to see its little face before it was born. I started to imagine what it would grow to be, who it would be, and with each passing moment the fascination just multiplied.

The Story Of The Blind Old Man

"Youth is easily deceived because it is quick to hope." – Aristotle

I prayed for a solution to my problem. It was difficult to concentrate on my lectures because I was so exhausted every day. My grades were good, but I knew I could do better if only I could find more time to study. I flipped through the newspaper every day looking for a better-paying job and I kept thinking that if only I could get a job in the field of information technology my problems would be solved. But no one was hiring, or at least no one was hiring people like me from Africa. There were plenty of vacancies, but nothing for a part-time student wanting to do computer programming.

Then one day a solution presented itself. There was a small advertisement in the newspaper, which read, "Blind, old man seeks live-in help, £100 pounds a week and free board."

My heart missed a beat as I read this ad. This was what I needed. I showed it to my landlord Daud. Daud came from Zanzibar and lived in a ground floor apartment. There were four male students from Zanzibar on the second floor and Mary, Sheila and me on the top floor. He knew that I was struggling to pay the rent; I owed him a hundred pounds already. After buying my books and stationery and paying for my transport, my original thousand pounds had soon run out. I went down to his apartment.

"Look Daud," I said excitedly, "I think I've found somewhere to live for free." He had become more of a father figure than a landlord really, and as he took the newspaper from me he shook his head and laughed out loud, "Getrude, Getrude. Remember, child, that nothing in life is free." He laughed down at me. He was a big man, broad-shouldered, and he stood head and shoulders above me.

"I'll call this man and go for the interview," I said. "I bet you I can get this job, easy."

"Good luck, and be careful," he cautioned. I ran to the call box at the end of the street to make my call for the interview. The phone we had in the apartment was a receiver only, and if you needed to make a call you had to go to the call box. I dialled the number and got an appointment the next day after college. I called WH Smith and told them that I had a cold and couldn't go to work that evening. My manager, Lisa, was very understanding, and she told me to stay at home until I was well. It was Wednesday, and she suggested I come back to work on the Saturday. That was perfect, it would give me time to pack and move out of Daud's apartment before the end of the week.

There were a few students in my class who had told me about alternative types of employment. Erica was a girl from Barbados and she had managed to find herself a rich old man who was taking care of her. He paid for her expensive clothes, fancy shoes, and even for her college fees, but this didn't appeal to me. If I was going to get this degree, it was going to be through sheer, hard work and nothing else.

The next day after college I got on a bus, and went for my interview. When I arrived at the bus stop the directions were simple and clear, and I soon located the old man's house. I rang the doorbell and he came out to answer it almost immediately. I remember thinking that it was rather fast for someone who was blind, but I soon thought that it was his house, after all, and he probably knew it very well. He seemed like a sweet, harmless old man who had a small dog as a companion.

As I looked around the living room he directed me into, I could see that I had a lot of work ahead of me if I got the job. The room was dark and the curtains were drawn. It made me feel uncomfortable. Why wouldn't he open the curtains, I thought? Then I remembered that he was blind, and he probably didn't even realise how dark the room was. The air was filled with the smell of tobacco and when I looked down at the small side table near his chair I saw a pipe, a bag of tobacco and a lighter on the table.

"So, how are you Getrude?" he said kindly. "Welcome to my home. Tell me a bit about yourself, and why you want this job."

"I've come from Zimbabwe," I told him, and I'm studying for a business degree at Southbank Polytechnic. I need a job to pay for my fees and books."

"And do you think this job is something you can do?"

"Oh yes," I said quickly. I wanted to make sure he thought I was capable. "I can do the job, I'm very hardworking," I said. "I can do anything you want me to do, I can scrub floors, I can wash windows, all you need to do is tell me what needs to be done."

"Okay, okay," he said, as he sensed my anxiety. "Let me tell you a little bit about myself." He settled himself comfortably in his seat and continued. "I lived in Africa for a while, and while I was there I contracted a horrible disease that affected my eyes, and so I lost my sight almost 30 years ago," he explained.

"What part of Africa was that?" I asked him.

"I was a soldier in Cameroon," he said. "I was stationed there for two years while I was in the army." We talked for a little while longer while he filled me in on his adventures in Africa. He gave me a lot of details and it did sound as if he had actually been there. It was quite fascinating. Then he showed me around the house, and he showed me the room I would live in if I got the job. It was four times larger than what I already had, with a big double bed in the middle and a desk in the corner. I couldn't believe that this room could actually be mine. We went back to the living room, and I sat on the edge of my chair, anxiously waiting to see if I had passed the test.

"When will you let me know if I've got the job?" I asked him.

"Oh, don't worry, I've already decided," he said with a smile, "You have the job, you can start tomorrow."

I couldn't believe my luck.

"Thank you, thank you," I said excited. "I will see you tomorrow." I dashed for the door, eager to go back home and pack my things. As I rode back to Vauxhall in the bus I watched the countryside flash past in a blur. I couldn't believe my luck, this was the break I needed – a paying job and free accommodation. I was also pleased with the thought of living outside central London; this concrete jungle that expanded as far as the eye could see had already started to depress me.

Nothing in life is free

When I got home, I went straight to Daud's apartment.

"Daud, Daud!" I shouted. "Guess what? I got the job! Free accommodation, can you believe it? I can live for free."

"Well Getrude, I'm glad to hear that," he said, and he sounded really genuine, it brought tears to my eyes. I'd miss Daud. He had turned out to be the best landlord a girl could ask for. He was also from Africa and he had lived in London for many years. He was almost like family to me now.

"Are you sure that this is a genuine offer?" he asked cautiously. "It sounds too good to be true."

"Of course it's genuine," I said quickly, hardly pausing to consider what he meant. Why are people so suspicious, I thought, why couldn't this job offer be genuine? I had been brought up to be positive about all things, and I thought to myself that this had to be the real deal.

"I wish you luck then," he said. "It's just that nothing in life is free. Are you sure there are no strings attached?"

"Of course not, Daud, he's a blind old man for goodness sake," I said, a little irritated. "What harm could he be?"

"Well, good luck, and if you ever need to come back don't hesitate to call me."

Daud offered to take me to the new house the next day. He knew I didn't have a car and I couldn't get on a bus or a train with my huge suitcase. That night I went to bed late after packing all my belongings. Mary and Sheila were really disappointed to lose me as a flatmate, but they understood that I couldn't afford the rent so they helped me with the packing.

The next day both Daud and Mary went with me to my new-found home. We rang the doorbell, and again the old man appeared instantly at the door. It was almost as if he had been waiting behind the door and it creeped me out a little, but I kept blocking away the uneasy feeling.

"Come in, come in," he said cheerfully. Then he stopped, as if sensing the presence of Mary and Daud.

"These are my friends Mary and Daud, they helped me carry my suitcase and belongings," I explained, seeing his hesitation.

"Oh, can I make you a cup of tea?" he offered. They thanked him and he went into the kitchen to make tea. While he was gone I showed Mary my room. She was absolutely fascinated.

"Getrude, you lucky cow," she said, "this is fantastic. This has worked out really well." She was genuinely happy for me and I dived on the bed like a small child.

"Free board, Mary, I can't believe my luck."

We went back to the sitting room to find Daud and the old man speaking in Swahili. He really had lived in Africa, I thought. Why had I doubted his story? After an hour of the old man's reminiscing, I could see that his memory of Africa was so sharp it made us all homesick.

Soon Daud and Mary had to go. I took them to the door, and they both hugged me, but as they turned to leave, a policeman appeared from nowhere.

"Excuse me, young lady?" he said to me. "Have you just moved into this house?"

"Yes, I have," I said proudly, "is there a problem?"

"I'm afraid so," he said. "I suggest you go back inside and get your belongings and get out of here."

"What do you mean? I just got a job here, I am working for this blind old man."

"We know," said the policeman, "we've been monitoring this house for six months now. This old man has had several charges brought against him by young girls from third-world countries who came here and whom he has abused. I suggest you go back inside, get your bag and get out of here."

I couldn't believe it. I stood in the doorway, too frightened to go back into the house.

By then the old man had got very suspicious. "Getrude, Getrude!" he called out, "who's at the door?" I didn't answer him; but turned to the policeman instead. I wanted to find out more about what he was saying.

"What do you mean I need to get out of here? I need this job."

"He's not blind, young lady. This old man pretends he is blind in order to lure young girls in." He saw me start in surprise. "Was there a lock on your bedroom door?"

There wasn't. I felt myself getting goose bumps all over my body. I had wondered about a lock on the door when I first went into the bedroom, but had quickly dismissed the uneasy feeling. There definitely wasn't a lock on my door. I felt the blood drain from my face and, seeing my worried expression, the policeman added, "I didn't think so. That's his game, he lures you in, he offers you work, and as soon as you get comfortable he will come into your bedroom at night and rape you. We've had three formal complaints against him, which is why we are watching him and monitoring the house. You are very lucky, and I suggest you go back inside and get your things and leave."

I started shaking all over, not believing the amount of trouble I had almost gotten myself into. I quickly went into the house, grabbed my suitcase, which fortunately had not yet been unpacked, and walked out. I didn't even say goodbye. Then the policeman went inside to talk to the old man.

Daud just said, "Get into the car, Getrude, let's go home."

I cried all the way home.

Do you believe in miracles?

"Miracles happen every day. Not just in remote country villages or at holy sites halfway across the globe, but here in our own lives. They bubble up from their hidden source, surround us with opportunities, and disappear." – Deepak Chopra, SyncroDestiny 2003

At the end of four months in London the strain began to take its toll, and I knew I couldn't go on the way I was going. I had to give up one of my jobs. I couldn't afford to live in the apartment either. Mary and her sister helped pay a couple of weeks of my rent but it wasn't fair to expect them to continue doing that, they were struggling students too. I could feel day by day that I was headed for a nervous breakdown. The WH

Smith job was the one that paid the most, and they allowed me to work weekends, too, so whenever I had the time I would go in and work. But eventually I had to give up this last job, it just wasn't working out because I didn't have enough time to study and my grades were suffering.

I had hit rock bottom. I ran out of food and I ran out of money. I was down to a pound of potatoes, and a can of corn, and I started going through my bag looking for coins so I could go and buy a loaf of bread. I sat on my bed shaking everything I had, my keys, my bedroom drawers, but I could not find 50p to go and buy a loaf of bread. I thought of calling my parents, but what could I say to them? I couldn't tell them I was stuck. I couldn't tell them the dream wasn't going to come to fruition, the guilt of having spent so much money, the last thousand pounds that my father had and which he had gladly given to get me to London, stopped me from picking up the phone and telling them that I was in trouble. So I rummaged through my bag and eventually I found 50p at the bottom of one of my purses.

Next to it was a business card from a Norwegian lady I had met two years before. She had come to one of our plays in Harare, where my performance had impressed her so much she had come backstage afterwards to speak to me.

"Hello," she had said, "my name is Ingeborg Tveter and I am from Norway. I just had to tell you that you are a fantastic actress."

"Why, thank you very much, my name is Getrude, very nice to meet you." I had replied and introduced myself. It was always very nice to get positive feedback from our audiences.

"Getrude, have you studied theatre?" she had asked, and I remember smiling.

"I would have loved to study theatre, but then what would I do with that degree? In Zimbabwe the performing arts do not make a decent living and I have to get a degree that will get me a job."

"Well, if you ever want to study theatre I will personally sponsor you," she offered. "You are very talented. Here is my business card. If you ever decide to take up acting professionally, please get in touch with me." I took the card and felt honoured that this stranger would offer such an opportunity. I thanked her humbly, knowing that although this was my dream it would never come true.

The strange lady turned to walk away and then she turned back again.

"Come to think of it, keep my card and if you are ever in Europe and you need help, I don't care where you are, give me a call." I kept her business card, put it in my purse and forgot all about it.

People talk about coincidence, but I now believe there is no such thing as coincidence. Everyone we meet, and everything that happens to us is predestined. I looked down at this woman's business card in my hand and wondered why I hadn't lost it. She had given it to me two years before and now I sat shivering on my small single bed, wondering why I had found it at that particular moment in time. Then I closed my eyes and I tossed the coin. Heads meant I would take the last 50p I had to buy a loaf of bread, tails meant I would go to the phone box at the end of our street and call this stranger and explain the situation I was in, and hope she might be in a position to help.

It was tails. I tempted fate and walked down to the end of our street to the old, dilapidated call box, dropped the last 50p I had in the slot and prayed she would be home. I dialled the number and someone picked up the phone at the other end.

"Hello, can I speak to Ingeborg Tveter?" I asked.

"This is she," came the answer.

"Ingeborg, my name is Getrude Bere, we met in Africa two years ago. You came to watch a play I performed in Zimbabwe, and you gave me your business card," I explained. I had to speak quickly in case I ran out of money. "The reason I'm calling is that I am in trouble. I'm in London and I wonder if you can call me back? I need your help." I gave her the number to the telephone booth and waited.

As I stood at the corner of that dingy street, the sun started to go down. It was the middle of winter, the days were short and the evenings were long. I started shivering, I had been in such a hurry to go and make the call, I only had my little red furry jacket on. I should have put on my coat, I thought.

Within a few minutes Ingeborg Tveter from Norway called me back. My heart missed a beat when the phone rang, but it was her.

"Hello Ingeborg," I said again more slowly, "this is Getrude. I'm sorry to bother you at this time of day but we met two years ago in Africa. You came to Zimbabwe, you watched me performing in a play."

"Getrude!" she said. "Yes, yes, yes I remember you. You're in London. When did you come to Europe?"

"I arrived four months ago, Ingeborg, but the situation I'm in now is that I have run out of all the money I had, I've been trying to hold down three jobs and that hasn't worked and I'm pregnant." I started to cry as I poured out my heart to this total stranger. "I've just got to find a way to get out of the situation I'm in. I know you said I could call you any time if I needed help, and I really do need help." And with that, the tears were uncontrollable. I think the toll of the last few months just hit me in one wave. She told me to take heart, and not to cry.

"This is such a strange coincidence that you should call me today because I was talking about you just the other day," she said. "My brother is currently working to bring together a group of people to work on a musical production about Nelson Mandela. The play is written by a Norwegian author and it's called Salt of the Earth. We need eight Zimbabweans, eight South Africans, and eight Namibians to work with a group of Norwegian students on this musical production." She paused.

"So, do you want to come to Norway? I could send you an air ticket tomorrow."

I could not believe my luck. This woman whom I had met briefly two years ago not only remembered who I was, she also had a solution to my problems. To take part in a play, and a play about Nelson Mandela, and to tour the whole of Europe with it felt too good to be true. Nelson Mandela was my hero and it would be such an honour to participate in something so meaningful.

"Yes, yes," I said quickly, before she changed her mind. "Yes please, I'll come, please send me an air ticket."

I gave her my address and sure enough the next morning a courier came to my door and there was my ticket to Norway, to do something that I loved. I made a collect phone call to my parents and told them about the pregnancy and that I was going to Norway. My biggest concern was my father's reaction but when he came to the phone he simply said, "Getty, just make sure you come back alive and bring our grandchild to us."

Heathrow Airport again, and I felt a sense of relief to be leaving this dreadful place. It had been nothing but an uphill struggle from the day I arrived, and as much as I had tried to keep myself excited about being there I had found it nearly impossible to survive without a scholarship, so I figured that if I went to Norway for a few months I could make a bit of money to take back with me to Africa.

The day I arrived in Norway, it snowed. I had never seen snow before. The whole time I was in London it was cold, bitterly cold, but it didn't snow. As we landed at Oslo Airport in late January 1989 everything was white, the ground was covered in four to five inches of this white powdery snow. I couldn't believe it, having lived in Africa all my life I did not even know what snow would be like. Ingeborg's brother, who lived in Oslo, came and picked me up from the airport. He hugged me tight when he greeted me, and whisked me off to his house to meet his family. As we drove away from the airport I asked him to stop so I could feel this wonderful, magical stuff that covered the earth in white. He found it amusing, and he stopped the car and let me experience the touch of snow for the first time. I have never felt more alive in my entire life. It was the coldness. There's something about being in a cold climate that sharpens your senses, and I just knew that this was going to be a wonderful and magical experience.

I spent the night at this man's house where his family was warm and welcoming. His wife and daughter were at home and their two sons were away attending university. The next morning I woke up and had breakfast, packed my bags, and was ready to be shipped off north by train to the town where my new guardian angel lived. The train ride was slow but very interesting. Ingeborg's brother had given me money so I could buy food and refreshments along the way, and as I left Oslo for

Tromso I looked at all the white covered earth and I wondered what the future had in store.

I arrived at my destination at 11 o'clock in the morning and there she was, the lady who had rescued me from the horrible drudge of London. Ingeborg ran towards me as I got off the train and hugged me like a long lost friend. It was as if she knew at that particular moment exactly what I needed. We talked for a while, she asked me how I was and if the trip had been fine, and I could just feel in my heart that I was in good hands. I was safe and everything was going to be all right again. She took me home, fed me and told me to go to sleep. We will talk in the morning, she promised. I slept a dreamless sleep in her house; I think it was just the fact that for a little while I could put my worries aside and rest. I didn't have to worry about where I was, how I was going to survive, pay the bills, or just get by. I could forget about all that for a few hours and sleep.

Fleeting angels

"A person is disposed to an act of choice by an angel ... in two ways. Sometimes, a man's understanding is enlightened by an angel to know what is good, but it is not instructed as to the reason why ... But sometimes he is instructed by angelic illumination, both that this act is good and as to the reason why it is good." – Saint Thomas Aquinas

I woke up to the sound of chirping birds on my windowsill. I thought it was amazing that any life could survive in that cold environment. I got up, had a shower, and went down to meet my hostess who had already prepared breakfast. But when I looked at my watch I realised that it was 3pm and I had slept for 14 hours. I realised then just how tired I had been – I had slept half of the day away.

When Ingeborg saw me, she immediately came forward and gave me a big hug.

"Welcome to my home," she said, "I live alone with my husband, you will meet him when he comes home this evening. All our children are grown up and at university." She explained this as she prepared breakfast, or was it lunch? I felt that I had lost track of time and I was very disoriented. We sat and caught up, and I filled her in on what a horrible time I had had in London and how relieved I was to have left it all behind.

"Don't worry," she said, "you will have a fantastic time with this tour. You're going to see the whole of Europe, you will go as far as the Arctic Circle with it."

"How long is the tour going to be?" I asked.

"Six months, but you can stay as long as you like. When you're ready to go home we will pay for your air ticket back to Africa." It was all too good to be true. Pinch me, someone, I thought, it was too good to be true. I asked her why she had offered to help me because I couldn't understand why this woman was being so kind to a total stranger.

"It felt like the right thing to do," she said. "It was the right thing to do."

This, too, was *Ubuntu*.

Salt of the earth

I spent an entire week with Ingeborg and in that week she drove me around to various places sightseeing. She told me that the town where I was going to work was extremely small. "Most of the people in Hamar have never seen a person of colour," she said, "so please don't find it offensive when strangers approach you to touch your skin. You speak very good English, and I suggest you give presentations about yourself. Go out and share your experience about living in Africa. People here will probably never get to meet another African person in real life.

All we see are the things on television, stories of famine and disease in Ethiopia. Remember that you are here to represent Africa, and make the most of it."

On the third day we went into the city. We walked down an interesting little market place where we found a woman selling a small African drum. I wanted it, not because I knew how to play it but because it was part of Africa, right there in Norway of all places. And as if she sensed my wish Ingeborg bought the little drum and gave it to me as a present.

"Use it," she said. "Play it, and this is one thing that will remind you of home." And it did.

At the end of my first week in Norway I prepared to travel south to the little town called Hamar where I was to spend the bulk of my time. This was where all the young people who had committed to take part in the production were living. The people of Hamar had collaborated to bring the group together to participate in this musical, and soon I was there too. It was extremely pleasant to see familiar looking faces and familiar looking people around me. There were some Zimbabweans whom I knew from way back home, as they were members of the Zimbabwe Association of Community Theatre. Then there was a group of Namibians and another group of South Africans. It was as if, after five months of being away from home, Africa had come to me. I was amongst my people again and we threw ourselves with vigour and energy into the production.

The author of the play was extremely impressed with our skills. Most of us could sing, some of us could dance and it was fascinating to see all these young people participating in this wonderful, wonderful activity. I got one of the lead roles, singing solo and dancing. The cultural exchange, I guess, was between us and the Norwegian students we were working with. A lot of them were young, aged from about 13 to 18, and as we tried to bring to life the sound of African music, so far away from home, we knew it was going to be a challenging experience.

In my spare time I discovered that, as Ingeborg had warned me, the people of Hamar were fascinated by the darkness of our skin. People would stop me in the street and touch my skin to see if the colour actually stayed on or came off. They would ask if they could feel my hair. I understood what Ingeborg had said and I realised that these people were actually willing to come and listen to me talk about Africa. They wanted to know things about our life so far away. And so I gave my presentation and people would ask questions like, "Do you eat cheese?" (Because they did) and "Where do you get your clothes from?"

After watching the media and the news, I knew why people were so fascinated. All the news on television about Africa had to do with the famine in Ethiopia, and all the images were of poor, starving Africans, without clothes, without food, without housing. When I tried to explain that we lived in houses very similar to theirs, we had electricity, we had running water in our cities, I could see the doubt and disbelief in their eyes so I took it upon myself to try and educate them that Africa was not all the same; there were parts of Africa that were well developed, there were parts of Africa where people lived peaceful lives. Soon the halls filled up to capacity when people heard that I was giving speeches about life in Africa, and I soon started charging for my presentations. I combined my information lectures with African storytelling skills and soon had a number of presentations to offer different interest groups. My audiences ranged from children to elderly people, and at the end of my stay I had put together enough money to buy all the clothes and other things I needed for my baby's arrival.

I enjoyed my stay in Norway, but after performing for only three months, I realised I had to go back home and face reality. It was the end of April. My stomach was growing bigger every day and if I left it any later it would be difficult to get a job when I got home. I had to go home, look for a job and try to find a way of surviving back on the continent. I explained to my sponsors that my time with them had come to an end and it was time for me to get back to reality. We had toured the whole of Europe with this theatrical production - from Norway to Sweden, Denmark and Finland. We even went as far as the Arctic Circle, to the land of the midnight sun and a town called Hammerfest at the far north of Norway. But I was four months pregnant and I decided it was time for me to go back home and look for a job before the baby was born.

Simbarashe – The Power Of God

When I got back to Zimbabwe it was difficult trying to fit in again. They say that once you have travelled you are never the same again. It was difficult having to answer people's questions as to why my journey had failed. Kwe Kwe is a very small town, the kind of place where everyone knows your name, and I had to learn to walk with my head held high and to focus on what was now my highest priority, my baby.

Barton was happy to have me back home and we planned our wedding. We decided to celebrate our union the traditional way, but I had never thought that our two cultures, Shona and Ndebele, could be so different.

Barton's family prepared the *Lobola* (bride price) for my parents, which included several head of cattle, two goats and a sum of money, and it was gladly accepted. Lobola is never paid in full. A son-in-law should always be indebted to his wife's family so that she has some security in case the relationship goes wrong and she wants to return home. Once all the traditional formalities were taken care of, we planned for the wedding. We would have two receptions, one at my parent's house in Kwe Kwe and the second at my in-laws' house in Shurugwi. I decided to make my own wedding dress, an elaborate white satin Edwardian gown trimmed with silver lace. I also made peach-coloured lace dresses for my 6 bridesmaids, lilac satin dresses for my 10 flower girls and white frilly shirts and maroon velvet breeches for 10 little pageboys. I enrolled in a cake-icing course at the local Polytechnic in the evenings, and made my own ten-tier wedding cake. My parents catered for 300 people and my father slaughtered a beast and three goats to provide meat for the celebration.

My grandmother came all the way from Wedza to be with us on that day, and other relatives and friends also came to share in our union. The first reception in Kwe Kwe went really well, although it was an exhausting day. The only thing that spoiled the celebration was that my grandmother fell and fractured her hip the day after the wedding, and she never walked again.

The second reception involved the whole village of Shurugwi, and we decided to park our vehicle 5 kilometres away from the house and walk. Traditionally the bride is completely covered in a white sheet and her future in-laws have to pay a lot of money to see her face for the first time. So with every step I took, money was thrown at my feet and all my cousins and sisters who were escorting me thoroughly enjoyed collecting the money. In the meantime all the villagers lined the street and there was drumming, music and singing to welcome the new bride and her relatives.

When we got to the gate, my in-laws had to pay a price to de-shroud me but unknown to me, my preparation for this event was not appropriate. In the Shona culture, a girl would work on beading a gourd with very fine intricate beads and it took about six months to complete this work of art. The gourd contained oil which I would offer to my in-laws the day after the wedding, together with a bowl of water for them to wash their hands before they ate the first meal I cooked for them. We do not use knives and forks when eating our meals, we use our hands, and they would use the oil from my gourd to moisturise their hands after they had finished eating. The new bride was also expected to bring a live chicken that she would slaughter the day after the wedding and cook her first meal for her new family.

When the sheet came off, there I stood proudly holding my gourd in one hand and a live chicken in the other, much to the horror of Barton's family. They are devout Christians and anything beaded was associated with witchcraft, while the live chicken was associated with voodoo and other rituals.

Fortunately for me, Barton's aunt was guiding us with instructions on what to do and what not to do. When she saw what I was holding, she came running out of the house and said, "Getrude, throw away that gourd, get rid of that chicken." And before I knew it, my poor little chicken ran scurrying off into the bush and the gourd was thrown into one of the fields behind me.

She later explained to me that most Seventh Day Adventists did not believe in mixing traditional African beliefs with Christianity, and had most of Barton's relatives seen what I was holding it would have spoilt the celebrations to follow.

And so I became Mrs Getrude Matshe. We went back to Harare and I started looking for work. I got a job with an IT company almost immediately, and we prepared for the coming of our baby.

In the meantime, my parents had started to get really excited about the coming of their first grandchild. My mother started knitting baby clothes and the house was full of gifts and toys for the baby. My brothers were also beside themselves at the thought of being uncles, particularly my youngest brother Tapfuma, who was only 15. Patricia was secretly hoping for a little niece, so all the clothes she made were pink. My grandmother, on the other hand, couldn't wait to see yet another great grandchild and didn't mind whether it was a boy or a girl.

When I first looked into his face I knew it was the power of God that had brought him to me, and as he looked back at me it felt as if we had known each other all our lives. And so my mother named him Simbarashe, which means 'the power of God'. Barton gave him his second name Sibahle which was Barton's second name too. This means in Ndebele "we are beautiful".

It was an easy delivery for a first pregnancy. The contractions started at 3am and by 7am on Monday 18 September 1989 I was holding my new baby son.

Barton was now a junior doctor and was on call which meant he had to stay at the hospital at night. Patricia came to spend the night with me just in case something happened while he was away. I had protested that I would be okay and that the baby was not due for another two weeks. After all, I had Angie, my fantastic young housekeeper. She was three years younger than me and she lived in. She became nanny and surrogate mother to my children and stayed with us for the next five years. But Patricia insisted on staying that night. I woke in the early hours of the morning to go to the toilet, and as I went back to bed I realised that my waters had broken, so I quickly woke her up.

"This must be it," I said excitedly. I had worked right up until that weekend, refusing to take the advice of all my colleagues to give up work and go home to rest before I had the baby. I was only entitled to three months paid maternity leave and I didn't want to waste a whole month at home before the baby was born so I stayed at work until the very end. Fortunately I was always active and didn't tire easily. If anything, I felt more energised towards the end.

We had already packed the baby's bag three months before, so everything was ready and waiting. I kept opening the bag every evening though, and I would hold up the little clothes and imagine what they would be like with a little person inside them. I couldn't wait any longer and I was good and ready to have the baby. The previous Saturday Patricia had organised a baby shower for me and invited all our friends to come and celebrate the coming of my new baby. The party had been a resounding success and I was overwhelmed by the number of gifts our friends had given us. Looking around at all those presents, the reality finally struck me. I think it was the high chair that Patricia bought. Once it was actually there in front of me I started to imagine our baby sitting in the chair and eating his cereal. I really was having a baby.

We tried to call for a taxi, but for some strange reason our phone line was dead. By then Patricia was panicking, but I felt strangely calm.

"Don't worry," I said, "Let's walk down the road and catch a taxi at the shopping centre." And that's what we did. I put on a coat while Patricia took the small suitcase with the baby's clothes and we started walking. It was a good 4 kilometres to the main road and I couldn't help but remember what my mother had told me about the day I was born. Unfortunately for me there were no caring villagers to walk with us to the hospital. City folk don't relate to each other that well and in fact I didn't even know the names of my next-door neighbours. But I wasn't in any pain or discomfort so I knew I would make it. Before we got to the taxi rank a police truck drove up alongside us.

"Where you going at this time of night, ladies?" the policeman asked.

"Please help," Patricia replied. "This is my sister and she's having a baby."

"Don't worry, we'll give you a ride," the policeman said. Patricia explained that we needed to go to the doctors' quarters first where my husband was on duty, so the officer suggested that she had better sit up front next to him and give him directions. That meant I had to sit at the back of the truck, and for company I had six large police dogs which didn't seem very amused at having to share their space. An iron grid separated us and, as if sensing my fear, they started to snarl at me. I had never liked dogs; my personal experience with them had not been good, and whenever I saw a dog I was reminded of the bites my mother had all over her legs. She got bitten when we used to go and sell our homemade wares in the white neighbourhoods.

My mind went back to my mother and I started to imagine how she had felt the day she gave birth to me. She always spoke so fondly of that day and I wondered if I would do the same for my baby.

We got to the apartment, knocked on the door and roused Barton, who opened it looking sleepy yet apprehensive. He dressed quickly and then we were ready to go to Avenues Clinic, the private hospital where we had booked to have the baby. The good thing was that at least Barton knew what to do if things went wrong. He couldn't believe I wasn't in any pain, as I was laughing and joking as if nothing was happening. When we went downstairs we discovered that our small, dilapidated red VW Beetle had a puncture. We called the car 'Things-Fall-Apart' because it was really in such a bad state parts were literally falling off it, but it was the only car we could afford. We went next door to wake up a friend of Barton's who came out immediately to help us. It would take too long to change the tyre so we decided instead to borrow his car, yet another old dilapidated VW Beetle although his was yellow. Fortunately the hospital was not too far away and before long we had checked in at reception and I was hurried off to the ward while Barton filled out the paperwork.

They settled me in bed and a nurse came in and ruptured my membranes, and I remember all of them laughing and joking about how long it was going to take me to get through my labour. "Oh, so this is your first baby," they said, and the nurse reassured me.

"Don't worry, it will take a while; just make yourself comfortable. I will be back to check on you in a while."

It was now 5am, and I had started feeling a bit of pain but nothing serious yet. Patricia fussed around me, anxious that our mother wasn't there to help me through this time but I assured her not to worry and said that at least she was there to hold my hand and we laughed about it. An hour later the contractions were still few and far between, and when the nurse came back to check on me she examined me and discovered that I wasn't fully dilated yet. She looked down at my feet and laughed, exclaiming that I would be in labour for at least 12 more hours if not 24.

Barton and Patricia were so anxious they started to make me uneasy, and when they realised they had forgotten to buy film for the camera I suggested that they go into town and buy some. It was early morning and they could be back within the hour. After they had gone, two nurses came into the room and began a private conversation, totally ignoring me as if I wasn't there.

"Ahhh, you'll have a long wait with this one," said the first.

"I know, this little one thinks giving birth is easy but look at the size of her feet. Goodness, she's got such tiny feet this is probably going to be a Caesarean section."

"Why?" I asked.

"Small feet mean small hips, and you are most likely not going to have a natural delivery," one of the nurses explained.

"That's right," agreed the other. "This is your first pregnancy; it's no easy ride, my sister. You could be in here for at least a day or two before you deliver." And with this discouraging news they left the room.

Thirty minutes later the labour pains became more intense. It was a quarter to seven in the morning and I could feel the contractions coming almost every five minutes. Before I knew it, it was every three minutes, then every minute. I rang the bell to alert the nurses that things were happening rather fast and they should come in and see if it was time for me to give birth to my baby.

Sisi, I told you, these things take time," the nurse said patiently. "Just try to get some sleep and I will check on you again in a few minutes."

"But I've got to start pushing," I said, "I can feel it."

She could see how anxious and distressed I was, and she came closer.

"Let me check again," she said, and she was horrified to see that the baby's head had crowned. She pressed the alarm and the older nurse came running.

"Sister, Sister, please come and help," she called. "the baby's head has already crowned." I could see that she was panicking. The sister in charge called reception and told them to call for my gynaecologist, Dr Kangwende, but he was too late. As he walked in through the door I gave my final push, and out popped my beautiful little baby.

"It's a boy," Dr Kangwende said. "Congratulations Getrude, you are now a mother."

"Thank you," I replied and I turned to the nurses. "Give him to me," I said, "please give him to me now." I could hear my baby crying, he had a strong loud voice, but his crying distressed me. All I wanted to do was to hold my baby and they appeared to be fussing around him, cleaning him up and taking a mighty long time to hand him over.

And then I held him. When I looked into his eyes, I felt we had always known each other. We stared at each other like reunited souls, and although he could not focus, I felt that he knew exactly who I was. I had always imagined what he would look like, I had started painting his little face the day I found out I was pregnant, and now I slowly unwrapped the flannel the nurses had wrapped him in and I started counting his little fingers and then his little toes. Ten of each, they were perfect little fingers and toes. Everything was there. Then I started examining the rest of his body, he was the most precious little human being ever created and he was mine, he was finally here.

When Barton came back I was holding our baby. Like me, he had to undo the wrapper and examine his son, and like me he was fascinated and thrilled that we had created this perfect little human being who was now part of our lives.

Simba was a peaceful child; he never used to cry a lot. When he was fed and his nappy was dry, he was the most contented little baby ever. I remembered my mother's advice when I was pregnant. She always used to stress the importance of being at peace with yourself during pregnancy.

"If you're miserable," she said, "You will give birth to a miserable child. If you cry or if you're angry, you'll give birth to a crying, angry baby." And so I tried hard not to stress and fuss while I was pregnant.

Time passed quickly after Simbarashe was born. He started smiling when he was two or three days old. It was very strange. He always used to look up at the floral curtain in the bedroom and focus on the top right-hand corner of the window and then he would smile. The first time it happened I thought it was a coincidence, but then it happened again and again and again. Barton was watching him while I had a bath on the first Saturday morning after Simba was born, and he said it had happened again.

"Maybe he sees his guardian angel," Barton said.

"Maybe he sees things that we don't see," I replied, a bit concerned, and I often wondered if that was really the truth.

Simba started to sit up, and before we knew it he could crawl, and before I was ready for it at nine months he took his first step. It was a bit of a shock for me, to be quite honest, and I was quite upset. Barton came home from work and found me in tears.

"What's wrong?" he asked. "Is something wrong with the baby?"

"No," I said tearfully.

"So why are you crying?"

"He started walking," I sobbed. "Simba started walking today and it feels like he doesn't need me any more." Now the tears were uncontrollable, and Barton laughed at me. I couldn't explain how I felt. It sounded ridiculous to say it out loud but when I came home that day Simba wouldn't sit on my lap for five minutes. I had spent the whole day at work thinking about my baby, and in the evening when I got home he didn't pay any attention to me. I guess what made it worse was the realisation that this was the beginning of the end. He had started walking and for me that signified that he had started walking away from me, and there was nothing I could do about it. Funnily enough I felt the same way when he got his driver's licence 16 years later.

By the age of three Simbarashe had developed into an extremely active and inquisitive little boy. He loved to dance and he loved to sing. There were days when Michael Jackson was on TV and little Simba would jump onto the coffee table and dance, trying desperately to be like Michael Jackson. His artistic skills developed very early too. I remember the first picture he brought home from kindergarten and how proud he was of his work.

"You're going to be an artist," I said. I had always imagined that my son's long slim hands were those of an artist, and deep down I hoped he would be a musician, perhaps a pianist, or a saxophone player. But time will tell.

Born on the Continent

Ziyanda – The Blessings Are Increasing

Two years later we were blessed with another baby. It was a girl this time, which was perfect because now we had our pigeon pair. She was born on the 16 September 1991, two days before Simba's birthday. What a coincidence. We named her Ziyanda Nothobeka, and her names mean 'the blessings are increasing' and 'the peaceful one'. The blessings truly were increasing, as she was a perfect peaceful baby girl.

She was born on a Tuesday evening, I had gone to work as usual trying to work to the very end of my pregnancy so that I could spend a full three months with my new baby. It had been an exhausting day and the elevator in our five story office block had broken down. I had walked up five floors that morning and was exhausted by the time I got to my desk, I was 36 weeks pregnant and expecting the baby in two weeks time. I dared not go for lunch that day and my friends went out and bought some food for me. In the evening the elevator still had not been repaired but the walk down the stairs was not as bad as going up.

When I finally got home I was exhausted and after having a quick meal I went to bed. It was 10pm when the labour started. At first I thought I had heartburn and tried to go back to sleep. After an hour I realised that I was probably in labour and called Barton to the bedroom. He was still in the living room watching TV with my brother Joe. Joe had been living with us while he finished his A level exams, his dream was to go to university and study law.

"I think the baby is coming", I called to Barton from the bedroom; within minutes both Barton and Joe were at the door. Joe was panicking while Barton on the other hand was as cool as ever, it takes a lot to fluster my husband.

"Is your bag packed?" he asked.

"Yes, it's all packed and it's in the wardrobe. By this time Joe was beside himself.

"Hurry up Barton, get the car", he said, "I'll carry Getty, get the car". He bent down over me ready to pick me up, but I brushed him off and told him I could walk. His fussing was making me anxious.

"Just get the bag, Joe, its going to be alright. Come on, get the bag and let's go to the hospital." I then remembered my baby; our live in housekeeper and Nanny Angie would look after him so I knew he was in good hands. Poor little thing, he was turning two years on Thursday and I wouldn't be there.

"Wake Angie up", I told Joe, "and tell her we are going to the hospital". I walked into Simba's room, he was fast asleep and wasn't even aware of what was going on. I kissed his brow and closed the door.

The ride to the hospital seemed to take forever, the contractions were coming fast and hard and this time I knew exactly what to expect. I didn't expect things to happen so fast though for as soon as I was settled in a bed in the labour ward, I was ready to push. It was good having Barton there this time; it had upset me that he had missed the birth of our first child. I kept thinking of how happy Patricia would be this time, all the pretty pink clothes that she had made for Simba could finally be used.

Ziyanda was born at 11.45pm, on the 16th September 1991. She was the most beautiful little baby girl and big. She weighed 3.4kg and was just exquisite. She didn't cry much like most babies do at birth; once she was out she seemed content and peaceful as if knowing she was in safe hands. Barton was thrilled and my bother would not control his joy, he ran into the corridor and screamed waking up half the hospital with his excitement. I fell asleep that night holding my baby girl and feeling extremely content, now my son had a sister and somehow that gave me peace. He had a sister; he now had one of his own.

We named her Ziyanda; it was a name we had decided on soon after we discovered that the baby was a girl. My sister-in-law had always said that if she had another child she would call the child Ziyanda. It was a beautiful name and very fitting of her character, I'm not sure what comes first the name or the personality, but she seemed to grow into her name perfectly.

When she was small she was a chubby little thing, with very fat cheeks and a very small nose. Most of our friends laughed and called her ugly but we didn't see it at all. To us she was beautiful. By the time she was 4 months they all had to swallow their words for she had blossomed into the prettiest little girl ever. She had thick, jet-black hair that grew so long that whenever I combed it out into an Afro she looked like Don King. I loved doing her hair and I learned new and innovative hairstyles. It was like having a baby doll to dress up in ribbons and frills.

By the time she was one year old her personality developed very fast, she was bossy and a true organiser, she loved putting thing in order and would spend the whole day stacking books, putting way all her toys and just basically organising. She was a real busy little body.

I had started sewing again to supplement my wages. I made wedding dresses and clothes for special occasions and I refined my design skills. Although I had no formal training in sewing, I had learned through observation in my mother's shop. She had employed three fantastic tailors from Malawi who taught me everything about dressmaking.

My children were peaceful babies but when Simba was three and Ziyanda one, I had to find a way of entertaining them while I worked. We couldn't afford a playpen so I found a large cardboard box to put them in. I would fill it with toys and books and they would play in there for long periods of time together so long as they could see that I was there. Ziyanda loved books; she enjoyed our reading sessions; so much so it didn't take her long to read when she reached the age of three. She is still a bookworm today.

My daughter is a very attractive girl. She looks nothing like me, more like her paternal grandmother. It was a pleasure to watch Barton playing with the children when he came home from work. He would spend hours playing with Ziyanda and they formed a special bond with each other. It reminds me so much of the special closeness I have with my own father, and I am so glad for my daughter. We had purchased a second-hand video camera at and auction and Barton would spend hours filming the children while they played and it is wonderful watching all that video footage now that they have grown up.

I see so much of myself in Ziyanda that it sometimes shocks me. She is passionate about everything she does and has fantastic organisational skills. Simba soon grew a tail though, and she would follow her brother everywhere, running after him with her short fat stubby little legs. He always ran fast ahead of her, never giving her a chance to catch up, but this did not stop her. My children grew very close. Their relationship cemented at a very early age, and even now that they are teenagers I'm proud to say they are very good friends.

When Ziyanda turned one, my grandmother came to visit us. It was always an honour to have her come and stay, for she normally went to my parents if she came from Wedza to visit, and we would have to go to Kwe Kwe to see her. This visit was very special though. All her grandchildren were arguing and debating where she should stay but she put her foot down and said she wanted to see me. She had never walked again after her fall at our wedding and she was always frustrated because she couldn't get around easily. Wheelchairs or crutches were not an option in her village environment so she learned to move along using her body and arms. She was a strong, independent woman.

She spent two weeks with us before insisting that she wanted to go back home. We took her back to Wedza but that was the last time I saw her again for she died in her sleep two weeks after her visit. I sometimes wonder if her insistence was because she had come to say goodbye to me before she died. The strange thing was that although I missed her I have never been able to cry. At the funeral I couldn't shed a single tear, all I felt was that she was at peace and she was finally able to rest.

Selling Snow To The Eskimos

My mother is the best salesperson I have ever had the pleasure of knowing – she could write a book on sales techniques. At the age of six I used to go with her whenever she was selling her handmade goods. She was a state-registered nurse, but to get us through our private school education she had to work extra hours, making products like doilies, tablecloths, hand-painted fabrics and cushions, and every Saturday and Sunday when she was off duty we would go to the white neighbourhoods to sell our wares. We travelled long distances on her bicycle. I was strapped on the back seat and on the front she would have a huge basket full of goods.

In pre-independent Zimbabwe, hawkers, as people trying to sell products door to door were called, could travel for hours before anybody would buy their products. My mother always used to say, "If you're selling, remember two things. The person you are selling to have two choices, they can either say yes or they can say no. If they say yes, celebrate because you have made a sale, but if they say no, don't take it personally. Thank the person for their time, and go and knock on the next door. Don't waste time thinking about the rejection because it really has nothing to do with you as a person, it just means that the person you were selling to didn't have a need for your product."

When we came back from the UK we couldn't afford most luxuries, and I still remember eating a piece of cake that was given to us by an old lady who opened the door when we were selling. We would cycle long distances and then walk between the houses, pushing the bike and knocking on so many doors, and on this particular occasion we had been to a good 50 households and no one had bought anything. We started off early in the morning and worked through to late afternoon and I could see that my mother was starting to despair. I was frustrated with all this walking. I was hungry, I was thirsty, I was tired, and no one would buy our products.

"Mama, let's go home," I said. "You keep knocking on these white people's doors and none of them want to buy. I'm hungry, let's go home." I was close to tears.

"We can't go yet," she said sternly. "Just remember that every time you try to sell anything; always come back with a sale. If you've knocked on 20 doors, knock on the next one; the twenty-first door might open." And that's exactly what happened the minute she said those words.

It was a beautiful, grand, white colonial house with large pillars outside the front door. I remember walking up to the front door and an old white lady opened it for us. Normally you were never invited into the house if you were a hawker. You would sell your wares at the doorstep if you were lucky, or people would simply close the door in your face without even acknowledging your presence, or at worst they would call their dogs. Dogs in Africa are used for guarding people's homes, and if the guard dogs were let loose on you then you would have to run. My mother has the scars of dog bites all over her legs to show for her selling years.

This particular old lady was special. When she opened the door she must have taken a second look at my sad, 5 year-old face, my dry, chapped lips and my hungry expression, because she invited us in. I had never been in a white person's home in Rhodesia before. She picked me up and put me on a chair, and before she even looked to see what my mother was selling she called one of her housemaids to bring a glass of juice. The maid came into the hallway looking flustered and holding the glass of cold fruit juice. Her employer's behaviour was not rational. I could see that the living room behind her was a mess; it looked as though she was clearing up the house after a party. There was a lot of food on the table in the sitting room.

"Here is the drink, Madam," the maid said. I could hear the voice of a gruff old man bellowing from the sitting room.

"Who is it, Agnes, who is at the door?"

"It's a woman with a child, bass," Agnes replied.

"What the hell do they want?" he shouted. "I'm sick of these bloody hawkers ringing the door bell trying to sell their crap. Helen," he shouted to his wife, "why are you letting these *Kaffirs* into my house?" His words were harsh. He pronounced his r's harshly, with passion, even anger, and I couldn't understand why he hated us. I had heard that word before -

'*Kaffir*' – my father had told me that the word was even worse than the word 'Nigger'. Why was he calling us that? We hadn't done anything wrong? My father said the word *Kaffir* meant an infidel or non-believer, but we were Christians. I felt my heart sinking. There goes our one sale for the day, I thought.

Fortunately, his wife felt differently. She offered my mother a chair as if knowing instinctively that she had been riding her bicycle all day with her load of produce on the front and me on the back seat. She got another glass and poured some juice for my mother. She then went to the table and cut me a slice of cake. It had been a good six months since we had got back from England, and in that time I hadn't had any cakes or biscuits. We had enjoyed them when we lived in London, but here they were all very expensive and we couldn't afford them. This was a slice of birthday cake, and she told me to eat while she talked to my mother. As she chose what she wanted to buy she spoke to my mother.

"Why are you selling?" she asked bluntly.

"For school fees, Madam. My two daughters go to the Dominican Convent and it's very expensive." Everyone knew the Dominican Convent; it was the best private school in the country. I remember the humble tone in my mother's voice; she sounded almost subservient. I hardly recognised the proud African woman that she was at home. Why was she acting like this? She didn't even look this white lady in the eyes and at that moment she and Agnes the maid could have been twins. It didn't make any sense to me.

"Why don't you send them to the township school?" the white lady asked.

"They need the best education, Madam. I am a nurse and my husband is an accountant who cannot get a good job, so I have to sell during my days off to make more money," my mother replied. In fact my father was working in a chicken-slaughtering factory at the time, because Rhodesia would not employ a British-educated black man with an accounting degree and he had to take whatever work came his way to feed his family.

"Why should they get a good education?" the white lady asked.

"To get out of poverty," my mother answered. Her reply was so simple it has been ingrained in my psyche to this day. I finally understood why we worked so hard – to get a good education and to get out of poverty. The lesson was learnt.

I'm not sure what it was that inspired that woman to buy from my mother that day. It must have been the replies to her questions that did the trick, but whatever it was it definitely worked because we went home having made our only sale of the day but with good money for it. The lady bought more than we anticipated she would, and it was actually enough money to pay for one term of our school fees. When we were leaving she told us to wait and she went back to the kitchen and wrapped up some of the leftover food that was on her tables. She gave us pieces of chicken, cake and biscuits; things that we couldn't afford to eat in our home. She packed the food in a small basket, gave it to my mother and wished us well.

As we were walking home that day, my mother taught me another very important lesson.

"Getty, always remember that there are good people and there are bad people in this world. They can be black and they can be white, and that white lady was an example of the goodness that exists in every human being." So I guess I have remembered that lesson, too, and I have gone through life looking at people in exactly the same way - not being judgemental, not stereotyping, not making assumptions about the people I meet, but giving them an opportunity to show themselves for what they are.

In 1993, Barton decided that he wanted to specialise and become a gynaecologist and to do this we had to leave home and move to South Africa. He applied for a place at university and at the beginning of 1994 we moved from Zimbabwe to Cape Town, South Africa. The children were aged 2 and 4. I worked for another year as a systems analyst, and at the end of that year I decided I wanted to go to university. It was a rushed decision – I just quit my job, came home and told my husband what I had done. Needless to say he was horrified, but I told him that I would go back to my sewing and make money from my sewing and dressmaking skills.

The day I was accepted by the university I was really excited. I remember sitting at the marketplace selling my clothes and opening the letter from the university. I knew it would be either an acceptance or a rejection.

It said, "Congratulations, you have been accepted for enrolment at University of Western Cape," and as I read the words my heart leapt out of my chest. I immediately started thinking, how the hell were we going to pay the rent? How am I going to pay the fees? I didn't have any money and I had just quit my job. Making this decision was the most irrational thing I had done in a very long time, but something inside me urged me on. It was the same feeling I had when I first went to London to study and when I went to Norway to participate in the musical production. I had learned to trust that gut feeling. Somehow I knew everything was going to work out.

It was not a very good day at Greenmarket Square. It was 12pm and I still hadn't sold anything. I put my head down for what felt like two seconds, and prayed. "God," I said, "you know why I've been accepted at university; you need to help me find a way to finance my way through it. I really want to do this. Help me find a way, amen." As I finished that prayer I looked up and there was a lady standing at my booth going through the clothes I had made. She was very impressed with the quality of my clothing, she told me, and when she spoke she had an American accent.

"Young lady, if I had time to try on these clothes I would probably buy three or four of your dresses, but I'm in such a rush there is no way I could try them on right now," she said.

"Where are you staying?" I asked her, because I knew most of the tourists lived in the local hotels around the marketplace. She gave me the address and it turned out that she was living at the University of Western Cape, the same university where I had just been accepted as a student. What a coincidence.

I told her that I lived in Bellville, which was about a 10-minute drive from the university.

"I could bring the clothes later tonight so you could try them on," I offered. We agreed on a time, and I remember packing up my things at the end of the day having sold absolutely nothing but for some reason feeling confident that this lady was going to buy at least one or two of my dresses so the day hadn't been wasted.

I went home, cooked supper for the family and at 6.30pm prepared to leave again to see this lady, whose name was Barbara Cambridge. She was from Dallas, Texas. When I got to the university she took me up to her room, tried on six dresses and bought four. I remember how surprised I was to sell so many dresses to her. At 180 rand each that was a real achievement, because normally I would probably sell one or two a day if I was lucky. My university fees were 4000 rands per year and I had just sold 720 rands worth of clothes, may be I could survive college after all I thought. I asked her what she was doing at the university and she said that she had come for a conference. There were 500 Americans at the conference in Cape Town, all African American with money in their pockets and no time to shop. They all wanted to buy something African to take back home.

"Why don't you ask some of your colleagues to come in and have a look at my clothes?" I suggested.

"Ah," she said, "I hadn't thought of that." I told her that I had everything she had seen at the marketplace in the car, and I could bring everything in for them. When we went down to my car to get the goods everyone was piling into the cafeteria for supper so I off-loaded all my garments into the foyer and Barbara shouted in her Texas drawl, "Hey, everybody, this young woman is selling African products. I met her at the market this morning and she gladly came over with some clothes for me to try on. Look at this terrific kaftan." She was already wearing one of her new dresses and she twirled around so that all her friends could see. "Come up to my room when you finish supper and buy," she told them.

God works in mysterious ways. She answers my prayers within a split second most of the time. The 500 American delegates finished eating supper, went up to their rooms and got their purses, and one by one they came to Barbara's room to buy. I sold 8000 rand worth of clothing and goods that night. My university fees for the year were 4000 rand so I had basically raised all of the money I needed for my first year fees, plus a little extra for transport and for food. I asked them how they had managed to come to the university and to live on campus during the holidays and they explained that there was a conference convener who scheduled all of these conferences, and that I should talk to them and see if I could sell again during the vacations. So that was my solution. I had found a way of financing my university fees by selling at large international conferences during the holidays.

It rains in Cape Town during winter, and the winter holiday in July was the longest vacation of the year so I couldn't even sell at the open outdoor markets then. This was the perfect solution to my problems.

For the next three years I got the conference diaries for the University of Western Cape and Cape Town University, asked permission from the conference conveners and sold my wares to the people who came to these large conferences during the holidays.

I discovered that they needed entertainment for their guests in the evenings too. Sometimes they would invite musicians, dancers, and all kinds of people to entertain the guests at night. I mentioned to one of the conference conveners that I was an African storyteller and a motivational speaker, and asked for the opportunity to come and entertain their guests.

"How much do you charge?" he asked. I closed my eyes and I thought of a number.

"1000 rand for a 45-minute session." To my surprise he was so pleased at such a low price he signed me up for three presentations that holiday so, combining my African storytelling and my sewing, I managed to pay for a three-year degree programme by entertaining and selling clothes during my school holidays.

It's surprising how when you really look for opportunities, they present themselves. While I was at university I attended a choral festival where the university students were performing and I realised that although they were all singing African music there was nothing African about their clothing. At the end of their performance I went up to their conductor and I asked him why the university choir didn't have a uniform. "It's too expensive," he said. "We can't afford to get a uniform at the moment." I explained to this man that I was a seamstress, I was a student and I made African clothing to pay for my university fees.

"What kind of budget could you work with, then?" he asked.

I said, "You tell me how much you could afford, and I'll make the clothes at that price."

He held a meeting with the students in the choir and a week later he called me and said they could only afford 150 rand per outfit. That was a lot of money for me, so I went into town and I managed to source the material at a discount. It turned out that he had 80 students in the choir, each needing an outfit, so I got the fabric really cheaply by bargaining with a West African trader I knew at the market and I got an embroiderer to do all the embroidery for me. I went back to the university conductor with a sample kaftan for the girls and a shirt for the boys and matching hats. They loved them and placed their order. I asked each of the students to pay a deposit of 75 rand to cover the fabric costs, and with this money I went back into town, bought all the fabric I needed. It cost 3000 rand and started sewing. It took me two weeks to make 80 outfits, but by the end of the two weeks everybody was ready to pay me the balance of the money they owed and I made 12,000 rand with this order.

The choir was participating in a national choral festival that year, so I made some business cards and gave five to each of the students. I told them that if anybody asked them where they got their clothes from, they should give out my business card. I needed more of this kind of work. The response was phenomenal and that was fantastic, because once again I had found a small market niche for my clothing. For the rest of the time I was at university I made choir uniforms with an Afro-centric flair.

Being at university was fascinating. I met some interesting people and I also realised that most of my lecturers were potential customers, so instead of taking one bag to college like most other students, I always carried one bag for my books and a second bag filled with clothing that I would sell during my breaks. I went from department to department showing the lecturers my beautiful African garments and they would buy. Soon the news spread that there was a student making clothing. Some of them placed orders for special occasions and I even ended up making an African wedding dress for one of the female lecturers. I made her wedding dress and her husband's suit. As I went from office to office, sometimes selling and sometimes coming home empty-handed, it reminded me so much of my mother and the lessons she had taught me when I was a child.

Born on the Continent

Dumisani - Give Praise

My last-born arrived two weeks before my final exams and we called him Dumisani Anesu, his names mean 'give praise" and 'God is with us'. It was a very appropriate and fitting name for the occasion, for we were truly grateful to have got through a difficult pregnancy.

When I was 30 weeks pregnant, I got a large order to sew 150 choir uniforms for children aged between the ages of 7 and 12. My stomach was getting bigger and as I got heavier and heavier it became more difficult to sit at my sewing machine late at night after college to sew. I persevered and made the 150 little dresses for these children who were going to Edinburgh to perform at a choral festival. The strain of sitting at my sewing machine making clothes was taking its toll, however, and I was hospitalised at 32 weeks when I went into pre-term labour. My parents came to Cape Town to be with us during this difficult time. I had to be hospitalised for two weeks; I had complete bed rest and I wasn't even allowed to get up and go to the toilet. It was difficult learning to use a bedpan. After two weeks I was allowed to go home and it was good to see my children again but I was instructed to stay in bed and take it easy.

That was not an easy thing for me to do. I have always been extremely active and sitting still is not something I do well. I had to lie flat for the next four weeks to try to give my unborn baby a chance to grow. The medication I was taking made my hands shake and I could barely hold a book, but I was very aware that my exams were coming up and I had to study.

At 36 weeks I went back to the hospital for a routine check-up. It was late afternoon and when my doctor examined me she smiled and told me that the baby was on its way.

"Go home and get your bag," she said. "You're already 4cm dilated and you might be holding your baby tonight."

I rushed home and told my parents, packed my bag and said goodbye to Simba and Zee. They were really excited about the baby and couldn't believe that when I came back home I would be bringing their baby brother with me. We went back to the hospital and checked in. The nurses made me comfortable and Barton was laughing at how smug I looked when I told him I wasn't in any pain and was excited that it was finally over.

"Aren't you feeling any pain?" he would ask.

"No", I replied, "it feels really nice to be getting this over and done with".

"You won't be smiling in a few hours time," he said.

"I know, I'm just glad it will finally be over, I just can't wait to hold this baby". I was truly just glad that it would finally be over.

My gynaecologist this time was a woman, Carol Thomas was her name and a very good doctor at that. She lived very near the hospital and when she was called for the delivery, she arrived in record time. The labour took a while though; the longest time I've ever spent in labour and little Dumi was born four weeks early, at a quarter to midnight on 17 September 1997. It was an amazing coincidence that all our children were September babies, born on 18, 16 and 17 September respectively, and none of them were planned. Dumisani was definitely the tiniest of the three. We watched the video of his birth years later and still marvel at the miracle of birth.

He soon developed into an energetic little boy and he absolutely hero worshipped his big brother. And just like Ziyanda he followed him everywhere. Ziyanda immediately took over caring for the baby and would insist that I strap the baby on her back when he was sleepy and wanted to sleep. She would spend hours with him and just loved being his caregiver. When he started to walk, he soon discovered that he was a little boy and that rough and touch games were fun. My two boys would play for hours and I sometimes felt sorry for my daughter for she was not a tomboy and would spend most of her time reading.

Dumi's first spoken word was "Simba". I had always hoped that he would say Mama but it was Simba who was the centre of his little universe. He turned out to be a very stubborn child and very opinionated and cheeky. He always felt he was right and would fight to get his way. We spoilt him rotten, all four of us, he was a precious little person and because we had come so close to loosing him, we let him have his way. Like his brother, he loved to draw; he always had his blank note book and could draw pictures all day. He was more passionate about his work though and is really quite a good artist. It pleased me to watch my children develop, they all had so much potential and we were determined to give them a life full of opportunities and choices.

People always say that Dumisani looks like me and that his good looks are totally wasted on a boy. I know that he has my eyes and my skin tone and he also has dimples on both cheeks. His hair was inherited from his paternal grandfather, for he has silky, curly jet black hair. My mother-in-law came soon after my parents left and stayed with us for a while helping me with the baby. It was wonderful to get so much support; she stayed for 4 weeks before returning back home to Zimbabwe.

I decided to have a tubal ligation six months after he was born because I thought three children were enough. I had made my contribution to mankind. And so I went in for the procedure and, strangely enough, I was extremely depressed afterwards. It may have been post natal depression, I'm not sure, but after one sleepless night I woke early in the morning and wrote a poem entitled 'I Gave It Up'. It seemed to help me cope with the depression.

I managed to get to the bottom of my depression and grief and to understand why I was affected by my decision. Growing up in the Shona culture I was socialised to the importance of having children, and although I have never considered myself a religious person, I am a very spiritual one. I had a very religious upbringing. My parents are Roman Catholics and my grandfather helped to build the first Catholic Church in our village. Despite all this my confusion arose from my cultural upbringing and the western beliefs I learnt from church and school. As a Shona girl I was told that if I died without a child I would be buried with a rat tied to my back, and that way my soul would be appeased and I would not come back to haunt my family.

As a girl I couldn't quite relate to this concept, but when I made the decision to be sterilised I grieved for days. The wrting of this poem helped me cope with the depression.

I Gave It Up

It's funny how despite the sense of freedom,
Of liberation, Of being in control
I feel a sense of loss; That precious gift I was born clutching in
my small brown fists
I gave it up for peace; For peace of mind
Which at this moment takes its time in coming
For as my body heals I cannot help but feel a sense of loss
For now my soul is weeping, I gave up a part of my eternity
The Part that made me whole; The gift of procreation
The gift that made me me;
It's an innate sense of being; a sense of purpose
It's funny how for some women this gift can be viewed as a curse
Each missed period the cause of days of anxiety and stress

Born on the Continent

Each missed tablet the cause of tension and distress
The fear of falling pregnant becomes a burden
And yet as I reflect I thank her for the gift
The gift of creation that was bestowed on me
As I look at my three beautiful children I feel blessed
That she chose me to be part of eternity
So now I soothe my aching soul and let her rest
For wounds do heal though spiritual ones take time
For as the flesh forgets so will the soul
For in each of my children I have left a part of me
They carry forward the genes that make me me
That small part is my eternity
I understand now that we do not die or go to heaven
We just flow on; on the river of life through our gene pools
As we pass on a little of ourselves we will exist in new life forms
Though when we come back we are not quite what we used to be
Through our children and our children's children
We will live forever and hopefully
Pass on the better qualities of what we were
So sleep my weeping soul rest now; we have closed a chapter of
our life
Of our existence for we are in control; we've taken hold
We've taken hold of our own destiny
We are finally in control

Getrude Matshe – 1997

170

On a rational level I know I did the right thing, however it did make me realise that I had given up a very precious part of myself. The whole concept of eternal life came flooding back and I realised that my children are my eternity. We don't die and go to heaven, we live on through our children and when I look at my children, the two sons and the daughter I was blessed with, I can see the reflection of me in them.

Both my boys have my big eyes, thick long eyelashes and oval shaped faces. My baby girl looks nothing like me but she has my personality. I see myself at her age and it sometimes shocks me to realise how much is inherited. I see now that I will never die – with each generation to come a part of me will live on.

After Dumi's birth I had exactly two weeks to prepare for my exams. I worked really hard and achieved my goal – surprisingly enough I got through every single subject, so I managed, as they say, to have my cake and eat it too. I had my university qualification, a Bachelor of Commerce degree majoring in Human Resources and Management, and I had my baby son.

Now it was time for me to go back to work, and getting a job after being out of the workplace for 3 years was not that easy. Most employers were looking for people who had experience in human resources, but all I had was my degree and my 15 years of experience in information technology. I changed my strategy and decided to target any organisation that could

171

give me the perks that I needed or was at least large enough for me to manoeuvre my way around in. The toe-in-the-door principle, my father used to call it. He always said that if you can't get your ideal job you should take the next best thing and choose an organisation where you have the ability to grow. I chose Old Mutual, one of the largest insurance companies in South Africa.

They had advertised for new graduates to work in their call centre for a new investment unit that had been formed. When I went for my interview I impressed them with my IT skills, and the fact that I had just completed a business degree was a real plus so I got the job. I started as a service centre consultant, answering phones in a call centre and advising potential investors on the best investment options for their money. My friends couldn't understand why I wasn't looking for a better job but they didn't realise how difficult it was to come straight out of college and get the perfect fit. I had to settle for second best but, after three months, second best turned out just right for me. My boss was a very intuitive man and he was so impressed, particularly with my IT skills that he called me in and asked me why I had applied for this particular job. He felt my skills were wasted sitting on the telephone all day, and so I explained my 'toe in the door' principle. He immediately recommended that I transfer to the IT department where I got a position as a senior systems analyst in the web development team. The move trebled my salary.

After working for Old Mutual for a couple of years I decided to challenge myself even further. I saw a job advertised at MTN, the largest telecommunications company in South Africa, and applied for the job as Systems Support Manager, Africa. I got the job and again doubled my salary, but it meant moving the whole family from Cape Town to Johannesburg. We got a house in Sandton, Johannesburg, and had to cope with a very quick change of environment.

Johannesburg is a large city with a lot of challenges in terms of crime and unemployment. We had to live as virtual prisoners in our own home, with burglar bars and an electric fence. After a year the strain started to take its toll and what made it really difficult was the crime. One day my husband arrived home from the airport where he had gone to pick up a friend, and while he was trying to open the electric gate to our property three men appeared from nowhere. One of them put a gun to his head and told him that they only wanted the bags that our visitor had. They had followed Barton and our friend from the international arrival terminal at the airport, 40 kilometres away, all the way to Sandton because they knew that a foreign visitor would arrive with a lot of foreign currency and valuable goods. My husband gave them the bags because he knew that if he resisted he and our visitor would have been shot. That's when we decided the time had come for us to go back home, so we packed our bags and went back to Zimbabwe.

We found that life in Zimbabwe had changed in the seven years we had been away. The economy had deteriorated, there was no fuel or bread, and basic food like butter and cooking oil was in short supply on the shelves of our shops. Barton found employment in Bulawayo at the local hospital but I struggled to get work. There were no jobs, industry was struggling and a lot of companies were closing down. I sat at home with the children going absolutely crazy. It was hard because I had never stayed at home before; I had been used to going to work every day.

The challenge of coping with HIV and AIDS was daunting. Farai and James had just passed away and it seemed that all our relatives were dying. It was not just the stress of coping with those around us who had HIV; it was that my husband was at risk every day he went to work. Barton was a needle-prick away from contracting HIV, working in a health system that had no antiretroviral drugs and in an environment where the health system could not test patients due to lack of resources. All that protected him were his thin surgical gloves and that wasn't enough for us.

For me and the children the risk of being raped and contracting the disease was high. Our traditional healers, whom many people turned to as a cheaper alternative to western medicine, were advising their patients that they could be cured of HIV if they raped a virgin. In an atmosphere of ignorance and lack of education this was widely believed, and there was

174

also a level of anger directed at those few families fortunate enough to remain disease-free. After six months we started to think seriously of immigrating to an alternative place, somewhere safe where we could bring up our children.

I will never forget walking those two kilometres through the graveyard after we had helped to bury Marissa and her family. We had to leave Africa behind us physically, and we had to carry it with us always in our minds and in our hearts. Although we had left home several times before, there was something about this decision which had a sense of permanency.

We decided to see if perhaps we could go to the United States or Canada so I went on the Internet and looked for opportunities to sell my African products in the USA.

I found the National Black Arts Festival advertising for traders to sell African goods at the next festival in Atlanta, Georgia.

Born on the Continent

Dare To Dream

If you have the ability to dream, and to dream big, the world can be your playing field. My mother believes that you should be prepared for all possibilities as you venture through life, so by the time I was 16 I had a driver's licence and a passport. Although I had nowhere to go when I got them, she used to say that at least I was ready when the time came. As it has happened I've lived a magical life, and all I ever wanted, everything I've ever dreamed of, has come true.

My first trip to the United States of America was to the National Black Arts Festival in Atlanta, Georgia. The festival attracts people of African descent and provides an opportunity for traders to showcase and sell goods from Africa. I arrived in Atlanta with $50 in my purse, one pair of jeans and two T-shirts because I had used all my luggage space for my goods. When I got to the airport in Atlanta, one of my bags was lost so I had to go to the lost luggage claims and there I met an interesting old lady by the name of Rosamarie. I remember reading her name badge and thinking that she, like me, had a misspelt name and there must have been a story there although I never found out what it was. Now Ms Rosamarie was a very special person. She greeted me and asked where I came from so I told her I had just arrived from Africa and that I was here for the National Black Arts Festival. She instantly took control of everything that needed to be done about locating my lost luggage. When they did find it, my bag was badly torn and Ms Rosamarie went and got me a brand new suitcase to replace it.

"Where are you staying?" she asked. I didn't know.

"I am going to try and find a cheap motel where I can spend the night and then figure out how to get to Clarke University tomorrow," I told her. She got out a telephone directory and started calling all the motels and hotels near the airport, looking for a fair price. When she found one she took me to a taxi, told the taxi driver where to take me and said he was not to charge more than $5. She knew that a lot of taxi drivers would take advantage of a foreigner who had just arrived. Before I left, she wrote her name and a telephone number on a piece of paper.

"If you ever need help while you are in Atlanta, Georgia, call me," she said. "Don't hesitate, just call me." I thanked her, slipped the little piece of paper somewhere in my bag and forgot all about it.

When I got to the hotel I discovered that the local calls were free, so I decided to try to wholesale some of my products. I woke up early in the morning and I got the telephone directory, went to the Afro section and called every African shop in Atlanta, telling the owners I had just arrived from Africa and I had some goods to wholesale. I invited them to come to the hotel to have a look at what I was selling.

Now Americans are extremely arrogant people and if you've got something to sell you have to go to them. I called at

least a hundred numbers and the reply was always the same –
"By all means, come to the shop and we'll have a look at what
you are selling." But I didn't know where any of these shops
were. Then I called a shop called Mutana and nobody answered
the phone so I left a message on the voicemail explaining once
again who I was and what I was selling, and inviting them to
the hotel to have a look. I left the details and my name and
phone number. By about six o'clock that evening I had called
well over 300 numbers but nobody had come to see my goods.

Sewing in Atlanta

Then I got a call from a man by the name of Matti Foncha. He
was from the Cameroon and he must have heard something in
my voice or sensed my despair, or maybe he had been in my
shoes at some stage when he first came to America, for he got
in his car and came to the hotel to see me. When he saw all the
things I was trying to wholesale, he said, "Don't sell anything
yet. I go to the National Black Arts Festival every single year
and I know you will make good money there. Your goods are
unique."

"But I only have $45 left and I have to pay my hotel bill,"
I explained. "Maybe I could get a job? I can sew."

"Right," he said, smiling at me. "If you would like to sew
and make some money, I have a shop full of fabric and I need

179

little girls' summer dresses. We will buy you a second-hand sewing machine and you can make some clothes for me at $5 a piece." The next day he came to pick me up and we went around Atlanta looking for a second-hand sewing machine, and when we found one I moved to Matti's shop and started sewing. He was leaving town the following week to wholesale his African products in other states, so he gave me the keys to his house and said, "Getrude, you need somewhere to stay. You don't need to pay any rent, here are my keys. I will be back in four weeks' time for the festival, so feel free to stay in my house." He organised with Mary, the lady who managed the shop, to pick me up and drop me off every day.

I know why Matti did this. He had come to the United States from Africa as a trader and he could relate to what I was trying to do. It is so important for those of us who have left the continent to remember where we came from and to lend a helping hand to others who are trying to rebuild their lives. To help them get out of the poverty trap, to help the young people get the education they so desperately need - this is *Ubuntu*.

I made 100 little dresses in one week. I made $500 and it was September and almost time for my children's birthdays so I decided to go shopping. Mary took me to a shopping centre, and told me I could call her when I was finished, but when I was ready I rang her on her cell phone and it was switched off. I tried her home number but it just kept ringing, so I went back to the shopping mall and started looking around again. I went back to the call box again every 30 minutes trying to get hold of Mary. I didn't know where I was staying because I had left my bag at the shop with the address to the house in it. I only had a purse with me.

After the fourth trip to the call box I realised I had attracted the attention of three strange men sitting in a car directly opposite the booth. They must have sensed I was in trouble, and before I could react they came out of the car and surrounded me. It was very hot and humid at the time and I was dressed in a short skirt and a skimpy top. As the sun went down I realised I must have looked like a hooker. The men started pushing me around in the phone box, calling me a bitch and swearing at me, and I remember thinking, don't say anything, don't say a word. If they know you are a foreigner they could bundle you up in their car, rape you, murder you, and dump you in a ditch and no one would ever know what happened. So I kept my mouth shut and when I got an opportunity I ducked under the arm of one of those guys and ran into a shop directly behind him. I could hear them cursing and swearing at me as I ran. They must have been high on something.

I asked the young lady who was in the shop for help. I told her I was in trouble and I asked if she could call a taxi for me because I needed to get back to the shop before it closed. She was a girl of about 17 and she started laughing and said, "Look, taxis don't come to this neighbourhood at this time of night. Where are you from?" I told her how I had come to be there and how Mary was supposed to come and pick me up.

"Is this Mary your friend?" she asked. "Hell, she can't be. This is a bad neighbourhood" she said. "Whoever left you there was either playing a very bad joke or they really meant to harm you."

"I'm closing the shop in 30 minutes," she said. "If you want you can wait for me and I'll take you back to the shop where you're working." So I waited for this young lady, and when she was done she closed the shop and she drove me back to Abernathy Boulevard. By the time we got there it was half past six and the shop was closed. I didn't know how to get back home and I started to cry. "Is there anyone else you know?" she asked. I couldn't think of a single soul who could help me, so I started scratching around in my purse and when I tipped it out I found Ms Rosamarie's number. She was the lady I had met at the airport the day I arrived in Atlanta.

We called her and I explained that I needed somewhere to spend the night. She didn't have a car but she asked the young lady I was with to drop me off at her house. "Just bring that baby girl home," she begged the young shop assistant. "I'll pay you anything, just bring her home to me." So the girl drove me to Ms Rosamarie's house and it felt like coming home. I spent the night there and in the morning we parted company at the railway station. She went to the airport to start work and I went back to the shop in Abernathy Boulevard where I had been working. My co-workers were horrified when I told them what had happened, but Mary simply shrugged and said, "I fell asleep." I realised then that my being in the shop had threatened her own position and she had meant me harm. It was time to move on.

I have come to realise that we all look to the heavens for God, seeking divine visions of our creator up in the sky, but what we forget is that God is with us all the time. God is the people around us and is in every individual we meet, and if you have the ability you can see; God is in every single face. A lot of people think that she is going to come down from heaven with a flash of lightning and a bolt of thunder, but that's not the case. God is people. I am God, you are God, and if you learn to realise and appreciate her glory and to appreciate and understand how she manifests in our lives, miracles can happen every day.

The producer of the National Black Arts Festival was Badi Murphy, he was also the producer of the New Orleans Jazz Festival. I had spoken to him before I left Africa about my participation in the festival. When I first met him, he was again one of those individuals I felt I had known all my life. He assisted and supported me during the 10 days of the festival. The festival was a great success drawing thousands of people everyday and my sales were good. At the end of that time I decided to extend my stay by another week so that I could attend a similar festival in Detroit.

Fortunately I had brought a lot of goods with me and I wanted to ensure that I went home with nothing but money. Badi referred me to a very good friend of his by the name of Zene Gibson, who was the most influential and well-known African American lady in Detroit. She introduced me to her network of friends of associates and I managed to sell a lot of my goods.

At the Detroit festival I had a booth in the busiest part of the complex. To my left was an African American lady selling T shirts advertising "The Nappy Hair Affair". This was an organisation that encouraged African Americans to keep their hair natural and not use dangerous chemicals to straighten it. We never really spoke to each other but she would greet me every morning when I arrived.

At the end of that week I went back to Atlanta, Georgia where I left the remaining stock I had in Mutana, Mattie's shop. He promised to sell the goods for me, and we arranged that I could come back to collect the money next time I was in the US.

When I got back home I was glad to be with my children again. I had really missed them and I realised that three weeks was an eternity in a child's life. The one who was affected most was our baby Dumisani. Patricia and I were separated from our parents for a year when I was small, and I didn't recognise them again for a long time. Now I knew how they must have felt. My biggest consolation was that I knew Barton had been there for our children while I was away.

One year later I returned to the United States of America. I remember speaking to my mother the night before I left and sensing her anxiety, because I was yet again getting into another aeroplane and travelling a very long way away. I assured her I was going to be okay, but she did not sound very convinced.

This trip included a stopover in Italy, and as we took off on the runway and started flying over the Swiss Alps I looked out of the window and saw the most exquisite scenery. I thought of my mother and how anxious she had been about my travelling. I wrote her a small poem that expressed how I was feeling at that time.

Swiss Alps – A bird's eye view
17/10/2000

I too saw GOD through fog
High up on high
Where clouds and mountain peaks do meet
And frozen lakes and icy falls
Are there untouched to keep
And crimson skies merged gently by
Where white clouds lie
And if I die my soul to keep
Please Mama, do not weep
For I saw GOD's majestic beauty sleep

The American Legion

This time I landed in New York City. I had made friends with a very nice lady by the name of Jade Banks and we spent the whole day wholesaling my goods in African shops. At the end of the day we had made $350. The next day I got on a Greyhound bus and headed for Mattie's shop in Atlanta, where I collected money owing for the goods I had left there the previous year. I then headed south, again on the Greyhound, to New Orleans to participate in the New Orleans Jazz Festival being organised by my friend Badi Murphy.

New Orleans was fascinating. For a whole week I was surrounded by jazz music. There were musicians everywhere and I lost count of the number of street parties I attended. I was a little shocked when I joined one procession in the street only to discover, after an hour of dancing and following the brightly coloured jazz musicians, that it was actually a funeral procession. New Orleans residents like to go out with a bang. I have never seen so many varieties of costumes, or so many alligator shoes which were dyed bright pink, blue, orange or green to identify the various bands.

New Orleans was an interesting city, old and steeped in history. The houses are old, particulary along the Esplanade and walking along the wide streets I could imagine horse drawn wagons and cowboys. The most fascinating place for me was the graveyards; all the graves are above ground unlike the graves in Africa. I couldn't help but wonder if that was why it was such a soulful place, all those trapped souls that had not returned to the earth. There were no ashes to ashes or dust to dust here because of the very high water table that prevented the digging of graves.

I sold a lot of my goods during the festival then I decided to go to Dallas, Texas to visit my baby brother Joe. Only now he wasn't a baby any more, he had recently married and settled in Dallas. I arrived at the Greyhound bus depot at Carollton only to find that Joe was not there waiting for me, and after an hour it was getting dark and the bus depot closed. I started to panic because I didn't know where he lived. Unknown to me, Joe was waiting at the downtown Dallas Greyhound depot.

A group of Mexican youths drove past, and back again, and I realised they had spotted me. Alarmed, I dragged my suitcases down the street and went into the first lighted building I saw. Country and western music blared, but as I walked through the door the music stopped.

"Well, look what the cat dragged in!" a male voice drawled, and as I looked around the room my heart sank. The room was filled with rednecks, loud, rough and definitely unfriendly.

"Is that the stripper?" another voice called, and they all laughed. There were no women in the room.

I went up to the bar and asked if I could use the phone. The bar tender jerked his head towards a phone on the wall and I went straight to it and dialled 911.

"Hi, I'm in a bar somewhere in Dallas."

"Yes ma'am, I can see that you are calling from the American Legion," the man replied.

"I'm black, and I don't feel safe here," I told him.

"I understand, ma'am," he said. "I suggest you walk out of the bar right now, and I am sending a squad car for you."

I walked out of that room holding my breath. No one said a word.

Within minutes I was sitting safely in a police car. "Didn't you see the flags?" they asked me. When I explained that I was from Africa and had no idea what the American Legion was they thought it was a huge joke. They explained that I had walked right into a white supremacist headquarters. They called Joe's home and his wife said that he had left his cell phone at home. He was with a friend whom she could call, and so we finally found each other.

My good friend Badi had given me a list of names of people who could help me to sell my goods while I was in Dallas.

One of them was Jane Williams, and I called her and introduced myself, telling her who had referred me to her, and asked if I could see her and get a few ideas on where I could sell my products. And so I went to see Badi's friend Jane and we discovered we had met the year before. She was the lady who had been selling Nappy Hair Affair products right next to me in Detroit. She told me that she had a friend who was a seamstress, owned a re-upholstery factory and would probably be looking for people to work for her during the Christmas season, and as I was keen to make money I instantly asked her to introduce me.

Going home another way

The day I met Mary Simms, she did not feel like a stranger to me. I can't explain the familiarity of her spirit but she felt like someone I had known for centuries. She was extremely business-like and curt, and asked me if I had ever used an industrial sewing machine. I had never touched one in my life but I lied. I figured that one sewing machine had to be the same as any other. She cut out some sample pillows and got me to sit down at the machine and sew, so I had to try extremely hard to hold on to this big sewing machine as it vibrated through my hands. After 20 to 30 minutes I had sewn up all the pieces she had given me and it seemed that I made an impression, for she offered me the job there and then.

The next morning, feeling victorious and inspired, I started working for Mary but after two weeks the commute between her factory and my brother's house became a strain. I discovered that Jane had a room I could use at the back of her house, so for $50 a week I lived in Jane's back room and because it was so near to Mary's she would come every day at six o'clock in the morning and pick me up for work. I worked in Mary's factory until the early hours of the evening because I knew that the longer I worked the more money I made. She was paying me piecework rates and that motivated me even more.

After I had been there for three or four weeks I got notification that a consignment of goods I had shipped from Africa had arrived in Detroit, so I had to go to clear it through customs and see if I could start selling the goods. By this time Mary had invited me to live in her house. When she discovered how much rent I was paying at her friend's house she insisted I move in with her immediately and she didn't charge me a cent. So Mary and I became really good friends and kept in touch as I travelled around the United States, and her home became my home away from home.

I guess what made the biggest impression on me was this lady's personality. When she told about the struggles she had gone through with drug abuse and how she had managed to change her life and get back on track, I felt myself drawn more and more to her. She had self-published a book entitled *Going Home Another Way.*

After reading Mary's book I decided that maybe I would publish my own book and, five years after leaving the United States and at a time when I was making critical decisions on launching my book and finalising the material, Mary came to visit me in New Zealand. We spent a month working and refining the material of this book and it is in print because of her inspiring spirit. She has the most incredible ability to manifest in my life when I need her most.

Now, let me describe Mary. When we first met she must have been about 45 years old and the thing that struck me most about her was her natural and exquisite beauty. I think what impressed me even more was her hair. Mary kept her hair natural, and I had just gone back to keeping my hair natural two years earlier. When we shared our experiences with our hair we realised that although we had led extremely different lives, the naturalisation of our hair had helped us to go back to who we really were.

For Mary, going natural had saved her life. Her addiction to cocaine and crack, meant that she found it difficult to sit in a hairdresser's salon. The sizzling sound of hot combs reminded her of her crack pipe and, incredible as this may seem, by not going to the hairdressers and by not processing her hair she succeeded in staying away from drugs. For me it was fascinating to realise that such a small thing could save someone's life. At least it seemed a small thing to me. I guess most of us have no idea what it is like to be caught in that trap where drugs take over your very being, where drugs become a way of life and tie you up in bondage and servitude.

For me, the naturalisation of my hair has been quite a journey. I had for years used chemicals on my hair to straighten it, and I had convinced myself that it helped maintain the quality of my hair and make me presentable. Like a lot of African women on the continent I used extremely harsh and dangerous chemicals. Surprisingly a lot of African women everywhere and not just on the continent have damaged their hair and have forgotten what their natural hair state is like in their efforts to conform. We try to fit in with what are seen as socially acceptable hairstyles in a world that is dictated by extremely Western images of beauty.

If you don't have African hair you probably don't know what I'm talking about, but our image of beauty has been women with bone-straight hair. And who are we trying to emulate? We forget who we are and once again we are in bondage to colonisation. We are tied to a belief system that dictates that women who are fair skinned are beautiful, and that natural African hair is dirty or unkempt. This belief system strips us of our identities because, as a woman, your hair is your crowning glory. Your hair is your tentacles to God. I never understood the Rastafarian belief until I went back to having my own natural hair again. Rastafarians believe that your hairs are your tentacles or your receptors to God, and keeping your hair natural opens you up to that spiritual being that is God. But at some point we have stopped listening, at some point we have stopped being, again we have stopped being African. I'm not sure what we are trying to become.

While I was in Dallas I also managed to contact Ms Barbara Cambridge, the lady who had shown me the way to make money in Cape Town. I simply looked her up in the telephone directory and called. It was good to get an opportunity to thank one of my angels personally. I went back to Zimbabwe having made a substantial amount of money, and I knew that I had a definite market for my product within the African American community.

I had also started teaching my art techniques in the community colleges, so I went back home and talked to Barton about the possibilities for us in the United States. We decided to go there with the children.

Born on the Continent

The Wrong Road Map

It was August 2001 and we were on our way to another airport, another city, another country and another home. Our destination was New York, USA and we were braced for change.

I had started teaching during my last tour of the United States. The community colleges were always looking for stimulating and interesting tutors to take lessons, and once I got myself established I was charging $50 a head with a minimum of 30 people per class. That meant $US1500 per workshop, enough to set us up in a new lifestyle. Now the children and I were on our way, while Barton remained behind working. The plan was that if things worked out he would follow and join us as soon as we were settled. I had lined up 13 fabric painting or batik workshops to teach people my unique traditional hand painting technique as soon as I arrived in New York.

We sat in the transit lounge at Johannesburg Airport, waiting for our connecting flight to New York City. We had left Harare at six o'clock that morning and we were supposed to have a one-hour stop in Johannesburg and then a 10 hour flight to New York. But it was already 9.15am and they had still not announced our flight. I tried not to feel anxious about the delay. This time I was taking my children with me and nothing could go wrong. We waited patiently as one by one all the passengers for South African Airways flight 7700 gathered in the transit lounge. We were all anxious about the delay and wondered why the flight attendants had not announced it was time to embark and continue on our journey.

Then at 9:30am, the announcement came.

"Would all passengers for South African Airways flight 7700 to New York please report to the South African Airways information desk. Passengers for South African Airways flight to New York 7700, please report to the South African Airways information desk."

I had felt uneasy about this journey from the outset and now I was even more worried by the delay. It's because I'm travelling with the children, I told myself, but the quivering feeling I had at the bottom of my stomach persisted. I put it down to nerves, but deep down in the back of my mind I knew that something was about to go wrong. Despite my decision to ignore my intuition, which by now I should have started to trust, I could not shake the uneasy feeling.

One by one we approached the information desk. The lady in front of me was a young African girl who was cheerful and friendly, and her greeting put me at ease immediately.

"*Dumela me*. Hello ma'am," she said in Sesotho, disarming all my fears.

"*Dumela*," I replied with a smile. I started to pull out our passports and air tickets from my handbag, but she stopped me and explained the reason for our delay.

"Don't worry ma'am; your flight has been delayed. We are issuing hotel and food vouchers for all passengers of South

African Airways flight 7700. I understand there are four of you travelling to New York?"

"Yes, I'm travelling with my three children. What has caused the delay?" I asked.

"All we have been told is that the aeroplane has developed a technical problem and the engineers are attending to it as we speak. We have been instructed to book all the passengers into the transit hotel for the night," she said. "You are now scheduled to leave tomorrow morning at 9:30am. Here are your vouchers for lunch, supper and breakfast tomorrow morning."

I thanked her and hurriedly moved aside so that she could serve the people behind me. I felt relieved that this was the only problem and glad that we would be safely on our plane the next morning. I looked around for a public telephone booth; as I needed to make a few calls. Jade Banks would be waiting for us at the airport in New York in the early hours of the morning so I had to warn her about the delay. I also had to call Barton and let him know, as he would be just as anxious as I was. He would call my parents and the rest of the family and give them the news; and hopefully the next morning we would continue on our journey.

Lost in transit

As we walked to the airport transit hotel I was relieved to see that the children hadn't picked up on my anxiety. We checked into the hotel and found it was a decent place. We had a large room with a TV, which kept the kids occupied for the rest of the day, and I tried to keep myself busy by reading a book and some magazines I had brought along for the flight. I still couldn't shake the uneasy feeling. What could possibly go wrong now, I kept asking myself. I had been in a variety of similar situations in the last six months as I travelled between the United States, South Africa and Zimbabwe.

I think at this stage I had managed to find and to trust my intuitive self. There was something wrong about this delay, something that made me sense an element of doom. It was a restless night for me as I tossed and turned, failing dismally to shake off my anxiety. The children, on the other hand, slept well despite the unfamiliar setting. I woke them up early at six o'clock and ordered breakfast, and by seven o'clock they were fed, washed and dressed and we made our way to the departure lounge. This was an international flight so check-in time was two hours before departure. I made sure I had all our documentation, looked through my bag for our air tickets and passports; everything seemed in order.

Because I was travelling with the three children I knew it would pay to be first in line and the same lovely young lady who had attended to me the day before greeted me again.

"*Dumela me*," she said cheerfully. "Did you have a good sleep?"

"We slept well, thank you. I hope all is well with our plane this morning?"

"Oh yes, don't worry," she smiled. "The plane has been checked and fuelled and is ready for takeoff. May I have your passports please?"

I handed her the passports and the air tickets and she examined each passport one by one together with its respective ticket. My feeling of anxiety had still not gone away but I kept telling myself I could relax once we were inside the plane. It would be better still once we had actually taken off for New York.

The attendant picked up my passport, stamped it and put it aside. One down, I thought to myself. She picked up Simba's and stamped it. Two, I counted, relieved that we were finally getting on the plane. Next was Dumisani's passport – three. Yes! We are almost there, I thought, and I was slowly releasing a sigh of relief when she picked up Ziyanda's passport. As she was about to stamp it she stopped, and I remember that movement ever so clearly. It was as if her hand was going down in slow motion to put the final stamp on, then it stopped. Her hand came down, but not with the satisfying thud I was waiting for. She picked up the passport with both hands and looked at it again. Then she turned it over, looked me in the eye and said, "I'm sorry, ma'am, there appears to be an error. I'll just call my supervisor, I'll be right back." And with that she disappeared to the back office. I could see her speaking to her supervisor behind the glass-panelled window.

The other woman was white, a stern-looking elderly woman with jet-black hair and far too much makeup. She had pale skin and bright red lipstick, blue eye shadow and artificial looking jet-black hair, and I remember thinking to myself that she should have toned down that lipstick. What made it strange was that she was no spring chicken and she had obviously just dyed her hair the night before. I tried to focus on the trivial detail of this woman's appearance because I could not imagine what was wrong with my daughter's passport. But then the young African woman came back with her supervisor, who did not introduce herself but just asked me sternly, "When and where did you get the visa in your daughter's passport?" She picked up the other three passports and carefully examined the American visas. Apparently everything seemed in order with them.

"These visas were issued by the American Embassy in Harare," I said as calmly as I could. "It was about two months ago. What seems to be the problem?"

"There is an error with the passport number on this visa," she explained. "It is strange, but the passport number is out by one digit. It appears to be a typographical error, but you will need to go back to the embassy and get them to sort it out."

"I'm sorry...," I stuttered, "I don't understand. Isn't there something you can do for us here, please?"

"No, there's nothing we can do," she replied. "You need to go back to the American Embassy in Zimbabwe to sort the problem out."

"Please?" I tried to appeal to the woman. "Could you perhaps call the embassy in Harare for confirmation that this is not a mistake on our part? There's no way I could go back to Harare, I'm booked on this flight and it leaves in two hours time. I beg you, please can you call the embassy and ask them to verify the authenticity of the visa?"

But my pleas fell on deaf ears. "I told you, there's nothing we can do," she repeated. "You have to go back to the embassy and get them to sort it out."

I tried another tactic. "Please can I see your supervisor, or somebody else in authority who might be able to help?" I asked as firmly as I could. By this time I was holding up the queue and I was aware of the impatient passengers behind me whispering, irritated that I was not doing as I was told. My children were getting anxious too, and Ziyanda was almost in tears. The woman made a decision.

"Okay, wait here and I'll see who I can talk to. But please stand aside so that we can board the other passengers."

One by one the other passengers were checked in and started boarding the plane, but an hour later we were still waiting for someone to help us. No one came. I went back to the desk and tried to appeal to the young lady who had served me the day before and she looked at me sympathetically but explained that the matter was out of her hands. There was nothing she could do and I had to wait patiently for her supervisor. Thirty minutes later I went back again to ask if anything was being done about my case. I asked to see the elderly woman who had insisted that we go back to Harare to sort things out and she came out of her office looking pleased with herself. For a fleeting moment I thought my problem had been solved but she gave me back all our passports and tickets and said harshly, "It appears there's nothing we can do from this end. You need to go back to the embassy in Harare to sort this out."

Something told me that this woman had done nothing about my request. It's very easy to tell when someone is lying, particularly if you know they have taken an instant dislike to you.

"Can you change our return flights so that we can fly back to Harare today?" I asked. My mind was racing ahead, planning the journey back to Zimbabwe with the children. If we flew it would take us an hour, and there were flights in and out of Johannesburg to Harare almost every two hours, but if we got on a bus it would surely be a 19-hour journey. It would also be a long, hot trip and the children and I were already emotionally exhausted. But she examined our tickets and shook her head.

"No, I can't change the date on these tickets. These are Apex tickets. You realise that, don't you?"

I knew exactly what she meant. Apex tickets were cheap and you had to travel within the stipulated dates. The date could not be changed, that was the deal, and if you didn't travel you could not get a refund. Tears started streaming down my cheeks, I couldn't hold back anymore. Why had things gone so terribly wrong? Why would God let me get on the plane with my three kids and give me false hope that things were finally going to work out for us? We were in transit in Johannesburg, we had left Zimbabwe and now we had to face a 19-hour bus ride back to Harare. So I cried, and the children cried with me. I have never felt so helpless in my entire life. I could not control the events of this day and the thought of going back to the American Embassy made my stomach quiver. This was why I had felt so anxious about the journey. It explained the sense of foreboding I had from the time we set out.

I asked what would happen to our luggage as we had checked all our bags through the previous day, and was told that it would go on the plane without us. Now everything was on the plane and all we had were three small bags filled with the children's books, pencils and pens that I had packed in an attempt to distract them on our long trip to the United States. I waited in the departure line until all the passengers of South

African Airways flight 7700 had boarded, hoping against hope that the flight attendant I was dealing with would soften and allow us on the plane, but when it finally took off without us I realised that this journey was just not meant to be.

Back to Harare

I knew the bus ride ahead would be difficult. The next available bus leaving for Harare was at eight o'clock that evening and I had to think of what to do with the children all day. We could not spend the day at the airport and, unlike the previous day when the airline had graciously provided us with food and accommodation, I knew we were on our own. I had to think quickly so I pulled out my address book and scanned through the telephone numbers of friends who lived in Johannesburg. Then I went back to the phone booth I had used the day before. It was no use crying, I had to make the calls and tell everyone at home that our journey on to New York had not happened.

The first person I called was Barton and of course he was surprised to hear my voice. By now we should have been on the plane. Through my tears of frustration I told him what had happened and that I was trying to find a way for us to catch the bus that evening to come back home. He knew how important this journey was to the family and he tried to encourage me to be philosophical about the events of the morning.

"Maybe something would have happened to all of you if you had got on that plane," he said. "Look at what happened yesterday with the aeroplane needing repairs. Don't you think that is strange? Don't worry; just come home. Everything is going to be okay. We'll figure something out." But I couldn't stop crying, and the harder I cried, the harder my children cried.

"Mama, what are we going to do?" they asked.

"Mama, was it my fault?" Ziyanda asked.

For the first time I realised the full impact of the day's events on my children. Dumi was upset because he had missed his very first plane ride. Ziyanda was blaming herself for the error in her passport. She thought it was her fault we had not managed to continue on our journey. Simba, on the other hand, although as anxious and distressed as his brother and sister, tried not to show his anxiety. At times like that he took on an air of maturity way beyond his age. He would cope by withdrawing and not speaking or interacting with anyone. I knew my children well enough to recognise it was time for me to assure them that everything was going to be okay.

"It's not your fault, Zee," I explained firmly. "The error on your passport was not of your doing. We will go back to the embassy and they will fix it for us, you'll see. Then everything will be fine and we will make our trip to America sooner than you think." I tried to sound as positive as possible, even though all my optimism had vanished. Eventually I managed to call a friend. Mary's husband was Barton's colleague and they had gone to university together, and when I explained what had happened Mary immediately dropped everything she was doing and drove to the airport to pick us up. We settled the children and then examined the strange situation we were in. It was totally inexplicable – a typographical error on a passport visa? That was really bizarre.

We spent the day at Mary's house and in the evening she drove us to the bus stop, and so we proceeded with hope and faith on our 19-hour bus ride back to Zimbabwe.

I presented the passport to the US Embassy but, due to the ever-changing and deteriorating climate of our economy, the rules for issuing visas to Zimbabwean passport holders had been changed the week before. Staff at the embassy told me that I now needed six million Zimbabwe dollars in a bank account before they could make the change. We simply did not have that kind of money – we had just used all our savings to raise the air tickets for the journey to New York. I went back to the airline and tried to submit a claim for a refund for the air tickets but, as I expected, they refused point blank. They were Apex tickets and I had signed their no-refund disclaimer when I bought them. What a cruel game God was playing, I thought, giving us such false hopes of a new life in a new country. What kind of God was she?

Our bags finally came back to us, but the beautifully carved wooden bowls and animals and other local craft items I had planned to sell in the US were reduced to matchsticks.

One month after our ill-fated and unsuccessful departure was September 11, 2001, when America suffered the most disastrous terrorist attack in its history. I had been headed right for the heart of New York with my three children.

I remember at the time we were turned away from that international flight feeling as if my whole world had just crumbled around me. All I could think of then was that all the best laid plans never came to fruition. But when the twin towers were bombed a month later on 11 September I realised that I had definitely not been on the right road. That was not the path I was supposed to follow; it was definitely not on my life's roadmap.

Smiling through the storm

"Storms make oaks take deeper root." – George Herbert (1593-1633)

One week after September 11 I had a strange phone call from a friend who lived in Cape Town. Jesse sounded extremely anxious on the phone, and asked me if I knew that our house in Cape Town was up for auction. She had seen it in Sunday's paper and it was now Monday. With all the commotion, all the hustle and bustle and hurried preparations for us to leave Zimbabwe for the United States, I had neglected to monitor our bank statements and to ensure that our tenants were paying the rent. This was the only source of income we had in South Africa to service our mortgage, and to my horror I now discovered the tenants had stopped paying and the mortgage was three months in arrears. They had always been good tenants and had paid on time every month; however for the last three months they had paid no rent. When I called them their explanation was simply that the husband, who was the sole breadwinner, had lost his job and they couldn't afford to pay. What amazed me was that the bank had sent several warning letters to the house with regard to the mortgage and they had not sent them on to us, nor had they let us know that they were not sticking to their financial obligations to us, and now we were about to lose our home. Our house was on the auction list and we were about to lose our last precious investment. We had to go back to South Africa to try and sort out the problem.

Have you ever had one of those dreamlike and extremely surreal experiences of meeting an unusual and almost imaginary person? It happened to me on one very special occasion. I was sitting in the bank in South Africa, waiting for my appointment with a bank manager. I can't quite remember if this actually happened; my eyes were wide open and yet I feel that what I saw was strictly for my eyes only. I was facing a large revolving glass door where people were coming in and out of the bank. It was late afternoon, and it was easy to predict that the weather outside was about to change and there was going to be a thunderstorm. Then a strange old man walked in. He caught my attention because he was old and completely bent over with a hunch back, and his small figure was so distorted it was very noticeable. The old man saw me sitting in the managers' waiting area directly opposite the revolving glass door. He walked through the door, looked straight at me and came and stood in front of me. My initial reaction was to look up and smile. I actually don't know why I smiled. This was one of the worst days of my life and I still didn't know what the outcome of my discussion with the bank manager would be.

"Smile through the storm," the old man said, smiling back at me. "Just remember to keep on smiling, for if you do the storm will break, the rain will fall and it will wash away all your worries." He had a strange face, deeply etched with laughter lines and revealing a life filled with laughter. His eyes were the most memorable; they were deep-set and yet gentle. There was a surreal gentleness about his whole person, and to this day I'm not sure if I imagined this old man. I'm not sure if he really existed or whether he was just a figment of my imagination. Was he really there? Or was it my own conscience telling me how I should deal with this difficult situation?

The old man was bent over with age, he had a crooked back, and he said nothing to anyone else in the bank. He didn't even come in to do his banking. All he did was stand in front of me and tell me to keep smiling through the storm, and then he turned around and shuffled quietly and gently out of the building and back into the busy street.

When it was time to see the bank manager I pleaded with him and asked him to take our home off the auction list. I promised I would come up with the money by the end of the week. It was Wednesday morning. Fortunately for us we had left the house fully furnished so I had a large garage sale and disposed of everything we had and I managed to raise 2000 rand, just enough to satisfy the bank. The required amount to clear the arrears was 8000 rand and we did not have the money but I made an appointment to see the bank manager the next day. I deposited the 2000 rand in our account and asked him for a little bit more time. He was understanding and he gave me another week so I immediately put the house on the market. It sold that very same day so we managed not only to pay off the outstanding 6000 rand owing to the bank, but also to come out of the deal with an additional hundred thousand rand as profit.

Having accomplished the mission I started to travel back to Zimbabwe. I had to go 3000 kilometres to get home, but the journey back was quicker because I was light of spirit, and I had money in my pocket.

The night I got home I checked through my email and found a strange and unexpected message. My husband's cousin, who had lived in New Zealand for the last five years, had emailed me. I had last spoken to her a good seven years earlier at our wedding, before she left Zimbabwe for England.

She explained that she had been surfing the Internet and had stumbled across my email address on the hotmail address book. She wasn't even sure if I was the right person and asked if I could respond either way. I wrote back to her and we started corresponding. I told her we were stuck, desperately trying to leave Zimbabwe and were not sure what to do next.

At the time, every Commonwealth country was closing its doors to Zimbabwean passport holders, imposing visa restrictions and making it difficult for us to travel. Even though we had once been a full member of the Commonwealth, the political and social economic strife in our country had alienated us from the rest of the world. But my cousin told me to have faith. She said, "If you have the money, just buy air tickets and come to New Zealand. I promise you will not regret it." So in an act of faith, we used the money we had to pay for tickets. The profit we had made from the sale of our house ensured that we would land in New Zealand with a bit of excess money, surely enough to let us look for work and somewhere to settle. Once again we packed our bags and set off, this time to a small, remote island in the middle of the Pacific Ocean.

Born on the Continent

Aotearoa – The Land Of The Long White Cloud

We arrived in New Zealand on Tuesday, 2 November 2001. I was travelling alone with the children and Barton had stayed behind in case things didn't work out.

My cousin had advised us that I should come alone. She was a single mum with four teenage kids living in a small house in Karori. She explained that she could put me up on her couch, but if I brought the children it would be a really tight squeeze, so when I arrived at Wellington Airport I tried to hide three children behind my back. After everything that had happened I could not leave my babies behind this time.

She took us home, and as we drove through the Mt Victoria tunnel I looked around at all the strange wooden houses. They looked so frail and flimsy. Where I came from, all the houses were built with bricks and mortar.

We got to the house and settled the children and sat for two hours catching up on the events of the last 7 years. Then when we did get to sleep the children and I were so jetlagged we slept for what felt like two whole days. On Thursday evening my cousin came home after work and said, "Let's drive around the city and do a little sightseeing. I will show you the city and show you the different places where you might be able to find accommodation." We drove to the northern suburb called Khandallah. It is an extremely upmarket neighbourhood, and I remember her laughing and saying, "Look, you can't live in this neighbourhood straight away. It is very expensive, but at least this will give you something to aspire to."

I remember standing outside Harcourts, a real estate agency in Khandallah, that night looking through all the advertisements for houses that were for sale, or for rent, and studying the prices. As I was standing there a woman came out of the building and said her name was Trudy Flynn. I introduced myself as Getrude Matshe so we hit it off on our names. She was Trudy; I was Getrude, both variations of the same name. She was Dutch and spoke a bit of Dutch, and I spoke a bit of Afrikaans, so we struck up a conversation in my broken Afrikaans and her broken Dutch and became friends.

I explained to Trudy that I was new, I had just arrived and I was looking for somewhere to stay. She smiled and pointed down the road to a yellow apartment building.

"Do you see that apartment down there? That belongs to my sister-in-law. It is a three-bedroom apartment and it has been empty for three months. I'm sure if I put in a good word for you she will bring down the rent."

By the Friday after our arrival we had moved into Trudy's sister-in-law's three-bedroom apartment. We had nothing but the clothes on our backs and the apartment was empty except for a stove. My cousin gave us bedding and pots, plates and pans and helped us move in. Trudy told everyone in our street that we were a new family and that if anyone had anything to give away; they should come over and see me.

That Sunday afternoon my neighbours started walking down the street with a table or a chair or a couch, and by Sunday night I had a fully furnished house. It was as if my whole universe had just opened up and provided for everything we needed. We felt welcome, and I truly understood that a person is not a person without other people. Once again I experienced *Ubuntu.*

I bought Trudy's son's second hand car for $500, so on Monday I was mobile and ready to start looking for work. I enrolled my children in a small Catholic school just up the road, a three-minute walk from the house, and everything started to click into place.

The biggest difficulty I had was with Dumisami. He hadn't quite turned three yet so he couldn't attend kindergarten and I had to take him everywhere with me. I remember the frustration of trying to organise job interviews and not having anyone to look after him. For the first time in my life our children were my children and the weight of that responsibility and the knowledge that Barton was not there to share it with me made it hard. I had lived in a society surrounded by people, relatives and families, who would look out for my children at any time I needed them to. In that society, shared parenting was the order of the day. Now I was 17,000 kilometres away from home and I had three children to look after by myself.

Caring for the children

We knew no one but my cousin, who was working full-time to look after her own four children. I just could not get to those job interviews. I didn't have much money and I was scared that if I spent the money on childcare I would not have enough to feed the kids.

We were in the supermarket one day, at Pak n Save in Petone, when I bumped into a black Zimbabwean woman. She took one look at me and realised that I was from Zimbabwe, too, so she started talking to me and asked me where I was from. She had arrived in New Zealand a year before with her mother, her husband and their two kids.

I explained my dilemma and my problem with my three year old, saying that I had no one to look after him and I didn't have enough money for childcare. She said that if I trusted her she would speak to her mother and I could gladly drop my son off with her. They lived in Wainuiomata, so every morning I would drive all the way from Khandallah to Wainuiomata. I would leave Dumisani with her mother. The journey took 30 minutes each way, but our two families have become very, very close friends.

The woman who looked after my son is named Josephine and she took care of my baby when I went for my job interviews. After two weeks of job hunting I got a job in Lower Hutt working as a systems analyst for a company that designs hospital software. They didn't hesitate in taking me on, which was great. Most of the other companies had been frustrating to deal with as I tried to explain to people that there was technology in Africa, there were computers there, too, and I knew exactly what I was talking about. But this company seemed to realise the potential that I had, and after working three months I was promoted to a project management level and took over the implementation of a theatre system at a private hospital called Wakefield Hospital in Wellington.

After working for three months and facing the daily dilemma of picking up and dropping off children, my husband finally came to join us. It was a relief to be a family again, but he had difficulties getting registration with the New Zealand Medical Council so after sitting at home for a month, he decided to get a job in Mt Isa in Australia. He commuted back and forth between New Zealand and Australia for six months while he waited for his registration. When it finally came through he came back to New Zealand and we were reunited again.

I was barely managing to cope with the full-time job I was trying to hold down. I had to drive all the way from Khandallah to drop my son at Wainuiomata, go to work for the day, pick up the other two after school at five then get home and manage the household. I knew that the company needed me. They had given me a laptop to work on so I could do extra documentation in the evenings for them. I thought that if I asked them they might agree to let me work from home in the afternoons when my children came home from school.

Kukava Dacha kuriyambutsa
'To kick a frog across the street is to help it on its way.'

The morning I went in to see my boss I was extremely anxious. I had been there barely a year, and asking for different working hours was difficult.

"Jack," I said when I went into his office, "I need to re-negotiate my hours. It is just not working. I am running constantly, picking up and dropping off children. I need to re-organise my hours so I can work from home in the afternoons when my children come home from school." Unfortunately for me, Jack was not in a good mood that day. He was irritable and tired, and he just looked at me and laughed.

"Getrude," he said, "You have two choices. You either stay or you go." Most of my colleagues felt this constituted summary dismissal, and suggested that I take him to court. This man had put me on the spot and made me choose between my children and my job. But fortunately I had thought of a plan B. I had already decided that my children were worth a hell of a lot more than my job, and when I made the decision to ask to work from home in the afternoon I had already started formulating alternative employment options. I decided to go back to my painting and had already started painting metres upon metres of fabric to sell. I did a lot of soul-searching the morning before I spoke to Jack. I remember reading a passage in a book that said, "If man kicks you on the butt, let it push you towards your goal post." That thought came into my mind as I stood in Jack's office, shocked at his ultimatum. I thought, this must be the kick that I need. My goal is to be self-employed, to have the flexibility to pick up and drop off my children when I need to.

So I said, "Jack, thank you very much, but I resign."

When I got home I told my husband what I had done. Barton had been job hunting but hadn't yet found a job and he was horrified. He said, "Getty, what have you done?" I felt strong, however. I knew that somehow we would survive. The whole situation reminded me of Cape Town.

"I will go back to my sewing and painting and everything will be all right," I said, feeling full of confidence about my decision.

Unfortunately for me the fabric didn't sell, and after two frustrating months of going from shop to shop and from individual to individual, I realised I could not sell it to anyone. I had come from a country where everybody knew how to sew and everybody knew what to do with a piece of beautifully painted fabric, but here in New Zealand I just could not sell it. I had painted 300 metres of fabric and I was very frustrated, thinking that the little savings I had were about to run out.

Then one night I dreamt of my grandmother Getrude, my namesake. Now my grandmother is my spiritual guide. She comes to me in dreams and she came to me larger than life that night. She had her hands on her hips and she was angry. She was so angry and she was speaking in English and not Shona. She said "Getrude, if you have a problem, break it up into small pieces." I woke up suddenly and sat upright, trying to figure out what the dream meant. Barton asked me what was wrong and I told him I couldn't sleep and I had just had a weird dream. I looked at the alarm clock on the bedside table; it was two o'clock in the morning. I sat up for another five minutes trying to figure it out, but eventually I gave up and went back to sleep.

At four o'clock I woke up again and this time I knew exactly what the dream meant. I got out my scissors and I started cutting my fabric into small pieces and started sewing cushions and pillows. I made 1000 cushions and they started to sell. I saw a small vacant shop at the corner of the street in Khandallah village, perfectly located right next to the Post Shop. I found out who owned it and asked if I could lease it. I painted the building bright orange and filled the little shop with brightly coloured cushions, pillows and soft furnishings made from my hand-painted fabrics. And then my little business started to thrive.

That was in October 2002, and I sold the 1000 pillows in three months. People would come in and buy three, four and five cushions at a time as Christmas presents for their relatives and friends, and in no time at all I realised I had found a way to earn an income and to look after our children. My husband eventually found a job working at Wellington Hospital as a gynaecologist, and our world finally came right again.

Born on the Continent

Simzisani

My new venture was called Simzisani Creations, a coined name derived from Simbarashe, Ziyanda and Dumisani. Now that I was working in the shop I discovered that a lot of people didn't know who I was. This was a small community and so I decided to start marketing myself to the church groups, giving presentations about myself and making people aware that I was part of their community, in the hope that if they needed a present or a gift or just something unique to give away they would come to my shop.

People started to hear about my presentations and the invitations poured in. I started talking to an average of two groups per week, with roughly 30 people in the group so I would reach 60 people in the week. Before I knew it I was in the local newspapers and the number of people who came into my shop increased. I decided to put my business on the Internet, to sell or auction my pieces of work on EBay and other local websites like TradeMe. The bulk of my sales came from exporting my cushions and pillows to the United States.

I tapped into the African American web ring and started exporting my work to African Americans in the USA. I made good money on the auctions, selling cushions that would normally fetch $NZ20 for between $US45 and $US60. Soon there were hundreds of people bidding for my work, which was unique, as I never painted two pieces of the same kind. After doing this for a year I closed my shop and started working from home instead.

Medical Recruiters of New Zealand

During this time I started a second business. Through my husband's search for work I discovered that there was a shortage of medical professionals in New Zealand and Australia. He had found work in rural outback Australia and while he was job hunting we found hundreds and hundreds of vacancies for health professionals on the Internet, so I launched an agency called Medical Recruiters of New Zealand. The first five doctors I placed were friends - people we knew from South Africa who had heard that we had left Zimbabwe and were living in New Zealand. They were curious to see what it was like and before I knew it the business grew.

The most difficult thing was getting clients. Most of the large hospitals in New Zealand are run by District Health Boards, and they all had preferred-supplier agreements with large recruiting agencies so they wouldn't touch any of my candidates. I decided to go for the little man and I approached small, rural medical practices that were looking for doctors. This seemed to work and before long most of my clients were Maori health service providers in the North Island. I soon found a way of getting into the large District Health Boards too. If I saw a vacancy advertised on the Internet for a doctor, and if I had a doctor on my books whose skills matched the description, I would call the head of the department and tell them I had a CV for a doctor that matched their profile and ask if I could send it through. The head of department would then pass the candidate on to their human resources department for processing.

By the end of the first year I had managed to place doctors and nurses in all the country's 21 District Health Boards. I operated my business alone for the first year but it was difficult. It meant waking up at three o'clock every morning to go through the CVs that had been sent from overseas. Then I had to follow on with verbal reference checks and prepare their packs ready for submitting to the Medical Council of New Zealand.

My days were very long as I tried to stretch a 24-hour day to 36, so I decided to expand my team. There are a lot of former career women sitting at home in New Zealand with their children because they can no longer take on traditional nine to five jobs. All that was needed for my job was a good sales manner, a good telephone voice and access to the Internet, so I started a training programme to teach people to do what I was doing. From earning $60,000 a year as a systems analyst, I increased my income substantially and was invoicing an average of $20,000-$40,000 a month.

King Kong

In October 2004 I was at a presentation by Weta Productions who were talking about the making of the film trilogy *Lord of the Rings*. I had been an actress and I had always wanted to go back into acting if I could get an opportunity. When the speaker had finished his presentation I went up to speak to him and I asked how he was recruiting for the film industry. I asked if they needed actors for the new *King Kong* movie that I knew film maker Peter Jackson was working on.

He asked me to email my photograph and a small synopsis of who I was and what acting experience I had, and the next day he called me and said, "Getrude, how many Africans do you know in Wellington?" Now I knew about 50 African families in Wellington so I told him this, and he explained that they were looking for 350 Africans to take part in the Skull Island scene in *King Kong,* currently being filmed in Wellington. I explained that I owned a recruiting agency and asked permission to come and present a business case and introduce my concept for a talent agency. To my delight, they agreed.

That was on a Friday, and I now had an appointment for the following Tuesday morning when I had to present as many people as I could to Peter Jackson's team. I spent the whole weekend going from family to family taking pictures, weighing people, taking their measurements and capturing the data into a database of potential extras or actors for the movie. I knew that each family would know at least another 10 families. I travelled from Wellington to Palmerston North, Napier, Havelock and Hastings, and by the end of that weekend I had 450 Africans on my books. On Tuesday morning Simzisani Creations was reborn as a unique talent agency catering primarily for black African faces for the film and advertising industry.

It was fascinating how it happened. The casting director picked quite a few of the people in our group to take part in the Skull Island scene of *King Kong*. Unfortunately I didn't get a part because I was too fat and they were looking for tall, thin, lean people. My sister, who had just arrived in New Zealand from Africa, got a part however. She was so thin she was a perfect match for what they were looking for.

They filmed the scene in December 2004, and in January 2005 I got a call from Big Primate Productions again. This time they were looking for 450 Caucasians of Jewish and Greek descent in Auckland, and they asked me if I had anyone on my books. Now I had never been to Auckland except in transit and I didn't even know what Auckland city was like. I didn't know anyone there, but I sent out ten emails to people I knew and told them of this opportunity to work with Peter Jackson's team. After two days my 10 emails produced 1500 people of Jewish and Greek descent, all in Auckland. They signed up with my agency. The scene was filmed in Auckland and quite a few of our people got a role in the movie.

I Am The Wallpaper

I am the wallpaper
I am the distant sun
I am the blue sky around the clouds
I am the blackness behind the stars
I am the background that makes your foreground shine
One day the spotlight will be mine

I am the background to your foreground
As you are the foreground to my background
Together we complete

I am the backdrop
I am the dressing that completes the set
Aren't you glad we met?
Without me I bet
That shot...you could not get   Getrude Matshe – 2005

A month later I had another call. This time they were looking for 450 extras of all ethnicities to take part in a New York scene filmed in Wellington. Again I put myself forward for a role, and this time I was cast as an extra walking in the streets of New York. The original casting resulted in my getting two roles: the first as an uptown girl; the second one as a downtown girl. The uptown girl would have come from a fairly wealthy background. She would get to wear really nice clothes and have beautifully styled hair and makeup. The downtown girl would be a servant, someone from a very poor, low socio-economic background who was walking in the streets of New York after work.

When I went in for my wardrobe fitting, Peter Jackson had changed his mind. I was only going to take part in his movie as a downtown girl. I was highly insulted. I thought I looked good, and I wanted to wear make up and look fine on the big screen. I went home and I told Barton that they were crazy. Why had they cast me for two parts and then decided to give me only one part? Then after thinking about it for a few days, I realised that if there had been a black woman on the streets of New York city in 1930 and by a black woman I mean someone with chocolate brown skin - she would have been a downtown girl. She would have been someone of my skin tone, and I realised that I was here in New Zealand to represent that African American woman. So I accepted the role, and it was the best thing I have ever done for myself.

Now as an extra you have lots of time to sit around and talk to people. We weren't allowed to bring any recording devices or cameras on set but we were allowed to bring a book to read so we could keep ourselves occupied during the breaks. I brought a small notebook and a pen, and I would sit down and talk to all the strangers who were taking part in the movie. A lot of these actors were not represented by an agent and by the end of the two weeks I had signed up an extra 250 people for my agency.

I spent two weeks on set with Peter Jackson and I watched him work his magic. It was fascinating. We would walk on cobbled streets all day and by the end of the day our feet would be blistered. Our roll call was four o'clock in the morning, we would have breakfast at six and then we would be called up in groups to go and have our make up done and put on our clothes. Then all day we would walk up and down the New York streets of 1930. The set was beautiful. I felt as if I had stepped back in time to 1930, but I was right there at home in Lower Hutt, Wellington, New Zealand.

Participating in the *King Kong* movie made me realise the importance of extras in making movies. This is *Ubuntu* in a different context. Every single person is needed and has a part to play. Without all those background people the movie would not look real, and so they were just like the black sky around the stars or the blue skies around the clouds. Without the background we could not see the sun or the clouds. In the New York scene Jack Black, who was the star of the movie, runs across the road and hails a taxi. I was asked at that point to stand directly behind him and look longingly up at a dress on display in a shop window. So that was my role, to be the wallpaper or backdrop to the movie's stars like Naomi Watts, Jack Black and Adrien Brody, in order to complete the scene.

Behind the camera

By the time filming ended, I had decided I wanted to be a filmmaker so I enrolled in a course in TV and film production at the Avalon TV studios.

It was an intense, six-month course that taught us direction, screenplay writing, editing, camera work, lighting and sound, and in that six-month period we each got to make a small five-minute movie, a documentary and then our final piece was a 15-minute movie. I decided then that I wanted to be the first African person to write, produce and direct an Oscar award-winning screenplay. A lot of stories have been told about Africa and a lot of stories have been told about Africans, but never by an African person.

So that is my next mission. I have already started writing the screenplay. It is going to be based on this book and hopefully I will get an Oscar from the Academy Awards.

Wearing my father's shoes

A lot of people would describe me as being over ambitious. I've always had big dreams, and I've always felt I could achieve anything I set out to achieve. I guess growing up with parents who are big dreamers themselves, and growing up being told that I could achieve anything helped me to develop in such a way that I don't see any boundaries.

I remember at the age of six talking to my father and looking at a photograph he had of himself standing outside the Colosseum in Rome. He always used to laugh about that photograph. He would tell me that if I looked down at his feet I would still not be able to see that the shoes he was wearing outside the Colosseum had no soles. He had gone to Rome in the sixties, when Africans very rarely had the opportunity to get on an aeroplane, and his shoes had no soles, he had filled them with newspapers because he couldn't afford a new pair.

"All you need is a dream," he would say. "If you can dream, and dream big, your visions can become reality."

Herstory

If I could live backwards in time and see the end before I began, I would write my own obituary. The final chapter of my book outlines my dreams and aspirations and the way I want my life to unfold from this day on. I still have a lot I want to achieve, so here's to dreaming big.

Getrude Matshe was always her own person, startlingly independent, outspoken and challenging preconceived notions and expectations about her gender and her ethnicity. Her own life story includes many illustrations of her willingness to trust her intuition, even when it seemed to contradict what was expected.

This strong and independent woman was born Getrude Ruwandzano Muyaradzi Bere in Wedza, Zimbabwe, on 31 May 1967. Five children were born to Joseph and Evangelista Bere. Getrude was the second born, with an older sister, Patricia, and three younger brothers, Joseph, John and Tapfuma. Her sister describes the family's early years as 'well-off', which was not the life of the average African in Rhodesia. "We lacked for nothing," she says. In fact, the family lived in one of two houses they owned. "We worked hard though in those times. Everyone worked to put food on the table and to pay for our private school education," Patricia recalls.

Getrude Matshe learnt to knit, sew and crotchet at the age of 6, and by the time she was 13 she had started a small business making clothes for her high school peers. Her father Joseph was the first black Town Clerk in Zimbabwe, although he was not heavily involved in the politics of the day. Patricia tells of her father's rather sudden loss of employment, which may have been due to his lack of political involvement. When this happened life changed overnight, and at the age of 18 Getrude assumed total responsibility for the family.

Though so much of her young life was centred around her family, Getrude later revealed that she always wanted to see the world. During her early years she was fascinated with stories of other countries and had pen pals in England, America, Italy, Malaysia and Singapore. She could locate any number of cities on the map and explain the different cultural traditions practised in any given place. Her favourite subjects in school were English and geography.

Overseas experience

At 20, Getrude decided to follow the path that seemed to have been unconsciously unfolding throughout her life. She chose to go to England to pursue a Bachelor of Commerce degree, having corresponded and completing her A levels while she worked as a trainee computer programmer with Lonrho Computer Services, in Harare. In 1989 she began studying at

Southbank Polytechnic in London, far from her family and the life she'd known.

Despite the decision to begin her tertiary studies overseas, Getrude continued to value her humble beginnings in Africa and maintained close ties with home. Determination, self-motivation and drive were always a part of her life and seemed to stay with her throughout her days. Four months after landing in England, Getrude ran out of money and got an opportunity to travel to Norway to participate in a cultural exchange programme and a musical production about Nelson Mandela. The production toured the whole of Europe, including countries such as Sweden, Switzerland, Denmark and Finland. She returned to Africa after three months.

Home again

During the next three years, Getrude settled down and got married to her childhood sweetheart Barton Sibahle Matshe. They had two children, a son named Simbarashe and a daughter named Ziyanda. Barton was a medical doctor and in 1994 they decided to move to South Africa in order for him to pursue further studies and to specialise in Obstetrics and Gynaecology. A year later, Getrude decided to go back to university at the age of 27 to pursue her university degree. She graduated in 1997 and gave birth to her third and youngest son Dumisani two weeks before her final exams.

She had pursued every avenue to follow her dream of one day having a university degree. Despite limited financial resources she never doubted the direction her intuition was pointing her. She paid her way through college making and selling clothes at the local craft markets of Cape Town. She soon became a very well known and popular seamstress, designing ethnic clothes for the new African parliamentarians in the new South African government and later sewing choir uniforms for university choirs all over Cape Town. She started giving motivational presentations to various groups who visited the universities during the holiday, and offering her African storytelling services.

In 1998 she was invited to the Winds of Change conference in Sydney Australia to give a presentation on her life, and on the way back home she visited Malaysia and Singapore.

In 2000, Getrude and Barton returned to Zimbabwe and found that the socio-economic and political climate of the country had deteriorated. Getrude could not find work as a Systems Analyst and Barton could find work only in a government hospital earning a paltry salary. After a failed attempt to immigrate to the USA in 2001, Getrude and Barton decided to visit New Zealand to explore the possibility available to their family. Getrude Matshe never went back to Africa on a permanent basis.

In 2002 at the age of 34, Getrude launched her first business, Simsizani Creations. It was a small shop where she sold her hand-painted textiles and soft furnishings. She also sold a lot of her products on the Internet. In 2003 she launched Medical Recruiters of New Zealand, a large recruiting agency that now focuses primarily on New Zealand and Australian placements of medical professionals. In 2005 she broke into the film and advertising industry and re-launched Simsizani Creations as a talent agency focusing primarily on black African faces for the film and advertising industry. It is now Australasia's largest talent agency for ethnic minorities.

In the same year Getrude formed GM Global Investments, a property investing company that currently has a total portfolio averaging NZ $100 million worth of real estate.

On 19 April 2006, Getrude Matshe self-published a book that became an international bestseller. It is a spiritual memoir of her life entitled *Born on the Continent - Ubuntu*. The book spread the message of *Ubuntu* around the world. It has sold 100 million copies and is published in 50 languages. Her teaching was primarily compassion for humanity, in order to make this world a better place.

"If I could only sow the seed of compassion among people, then I could say I have left my footprint in the sand of time and my life would have been worthwhile," Getrude would say.

A movement begins – the Getrude Matshe Africa Aids Foundation

"If you find it in your heart to care for somebody else, you will have succeeded." – Maya Angelou

With the proceeds of this book, Getrude Matshe set up the Getrude Matshe Africa Aids Foundation, an educational fund to sponsor HIV orphans in Africa. The fund ensures that orphaned children get to university; education being the only way out of ignorance and poverty in Africa. Getrude formed the world's largest database that connects people who want to help people in third world countries, particularly children in need of education.

In 2007 Getrude retired, bought a luxury yacht, and sailed around the world three times. During her travels she wrote and later directed her first Oscar award-winning screenplay, based on her book *Born on the Continent – Ubuntu*. It has grossed 500 million dollars at the box office.

Getrude Matshe found a never-ending stream of human needs in the poor she met, and was frequently exhausted. Despite the weariness of her days she never stopped.

She was not alone for long. Within a year, she found more help than she anticipated. Many seemed to have been waiting for her example to open their own floodgates of charity and compassion. Africans scattered around the world adopted her philosophy to help at least one of their relatives back home in Africa. Young people from all walks of life came to volunteer their services and later became the core of her Foundation. Others offered food, clothing, and the use of buildings, medical supplies and money. As support and assistance mushroomed, more and more services became possible to huge numbers of HIV sufferers and their children.

From its inception, nourished by the faith, compassion and the dedication and commitment the Getrude Matshe Africa Aids Foundation has grown. New volunteers continue to come from all parts of the world, serving those in need wherever they are found: homes for the dying, refuges for the care and teaching of orphans and abandoned children, treatment centres and hospitals for those suffering from HIV.

"We are in the middle of a war, a war with the largest casualties the world has ever seen," Getrude would say. "We need to keep fighting to the bitter end."

Until her death in 2067 Getrude Matshe continued her work among the poorest of the poor, depending on God for all of her needs. Honours too numerous to mention had come her way throughout the years as the world stood astounded by her care for those usually deemed of little value. In her own eyes she was The Keeper – the protector of the innocents, the giver of hope, the energiser, the motivator and the comforter of the sick and dying. That was her life's purpose.

Despite years of strenuous physical, emotional and spiritual work, Getrude Matshe seemed unstoppable. Though frail and bent and with numerous ailments, she always returned to her work and to those who received her compassionate care for more than 50 years. Only months before her death, when she became too weak to manage the administrative work, she relinquished the position of head of her Africa Aids Foundation to her children, grandchildren and great grandchildren. She knew the work would go on.

Finally on 31 May 2067, her weakened heart gave her back to the force that was the very centre and the driver of her life's spiritual journey.

Thanks

Special thanks go to my grandmother Getrude Bopoto for all the love, affection you gave me. Your spirit will live on forever in my heart. I will miss you always.

Thanks you Patricia; for always being there for me. You are the best big sister a girl could ever wish for and I appreciate your undying support and love.

My brothers Joseph, John and Tafuma – thanks for being the cutest little brothers a girl could have.

Pricilla Muswibe, my wonderful cousin; thanks for the wise advice, coming to New Zealand is definitely something I will never regret. Thanks for all the support during difficult times.

My English teacher Dave Davies thanks for teaching me how to enjoy words, for showing me that English literature was alive and for making poetry so special by reading it to us as we lay on the grass in summer under the hot African sun.

Thanks to my very first angel, the lady at the student clinic, for hugging me when I needed a hug the most. For giving me words of encouragement when I was at my lowest and for passing on the message from my creator that everything was going to be all right.

To my Norwegian mother; Ingeborg Tveter. Thank you for being there when I needed you most, thank you for putting a roof over my head, for giving me peace of mind.

To Ngugi wa Thiongo, thank you for being the most exemplary mentor. Growing up in Africa and reading African literature has enriched my life. There's nothing like hearing about your people from one of your own.

To my roommates Mary and Sheila, thank you for being two of the most fantastic people a girl could live with. I appreciate your support in difficult times.

Badi Murphy of New Orleans, USA – thank you, Badi, for your guidance, for your kindness, for your advice while I travelled in the USA. You are a fantastic networker and I thank you for sharing your networks with me while I was there.

To Zene Gibson; Detroit USA, thank you for allowing me to be with you while I was in Detroit and for putting a roof over my head when I needed it.

To Uwimana Olibisi; Atlanta Georgia USA, you are one of those special, special women. Thank you for all the blessings – you know what I mean.

Ms Rosamarie; Atlanta Georgia USA, I may never see you again and you may never get to read this book but I thank you for being there when I first arrived in the United States. It was like meeting somebody I already knew, and I hope I will get to see you again in this lifetime.

Matti Foncha; Atlanta Georgia USA, for demonstrating Ubuntu. Thank you for your help and advise when I first arrived in the USA.

Ms Mary Sims, you know you are my twin soul. I am honoured to have met you. You gave me a home away from home when I travelled around the United States of America, and I am only glad that in this lifetime I managed in a small way to reciprocate the kindness that you showed me. Thank you.

To the old man in the bank, thank you for reminding me to keep on smiling - a lesson I will never forget.

Ms Barbara Cambridge of Dallas, Texas; thank you for showing me a way to make money during my university years. I know you don't realise what you did, you had no idea of the impact of buying four dresses from a young woman who was trying to make a living and go through college, but the timing of your visit to Cape Town meant I could obtain a university degree and I thank you.

Trudy Flynn thanks for being there when I arrived in Wellington. It's fantastic knowing you. The same goes to Helen Flynn. Thank you for providing the roof over our heads when we arrived in New Zealand. It was very much appreciated.

And a special thanks to my personal assistant Tania Palmer. Thanks for putting in all those hours and hours to type this book and for turning it into a reality. You have taken my words and you've put them down on paper, and for that I owe you.

Dear Reader,

If you have got to this page you have finished reading my book. I thank you for taking the time to do so and to contributing in a way to my effort to change my world.

If you would like to be kept informed about the Getrude Matshe Africa Aids Foundation, please send an email to Getrude@bornonthecontinent.com and I will put you on my mailing list and you will recieve the regular newsletter about the progress made with this book. My webpage is www.bornonthecontinent.com.

And may the force be with you as you try to change your world.

Much love, much respect

Getrude Matshe
Author and Motivational Speaker